C000112159

Book Design by Lara Sedaghat
Edited by Lara Sedaghat, Lillygol Sedaghat, J.W.

ISBN 978 - 0 - 578 - 90099 - 5

Before becoming enthralled by gang life, I was a kind, adventurous, and compassionate kid. In fact, as a boy, I would often come home from playing with some other kid I'd met hours prior, promising them food and fun at "my house." My mom would come to regard me as "always bringing home strays," and despite her interventions to prevent me from fulfilling what promises I made to any of my stranger friends by declaring "no they can't hang out here today," I'd insist that they "wait for me outside" while I had my mom make me something to eat. I'd then rush to reward them with half of my meal, and if they were to devour their portion before I consumed mine, I would offer whatever I had left. I was the kid who'd sneak you into my bedroom through the side window, where you could sleep hidden under my bed so you wouldn't have to risk going to your own home to be abused.

Long before developing a mature conscience to distinguish right from wrong, I naturally held a love for humanity--to protect, love, and bond with all people. I got plenty of whippings from taking food out of the house or sneaking people in, which I contribute to diminishing the

growth of love and compassion I had for people because the

pain from each of those ass whippings discouraged me from

extending the only kind of kindness I knew. I wouldn't be bold

as to say my mom was wrong for her method of protecting and

disciplining, because I am certain, had she known those

whippings imposed a confusion that facilitated a disconnect

from love for humanity in my subconscious, she wouldn't be

complicit. The very fact that she cared enough to attempt to

teach me by discipline is contrary to any intent to purposely

thwart my natural love to help others.

But while that may have been her best for those times, I

admit her approach caused lifelong unintentional damage.

Interesting is how my mother's best would eventually emerge

my worst, or as Lara would say, how this process of discipline

caused an "unlearning" of the natural desire for human

decency and a "relearning" of the unnatural thirst to kill, steal,

and destroy, a practice which has reinvented itself throughout

world history.

Although love is innately within us and will always be--no matter what we've done or what we've been through--there is something to be said about the importance and influence of one's environment, upbringing, and home life. Children are initially born as blank slates and each of those factors helps to shape the adolescent and the adult that the child eventually becomes. Love, safety, support, validation are vital for a child to receive as their perspective and connection to the world begins to develop. Parental figures are the first example and experience of love, connection, communication, coping mechanisms, ways of perceiving and interacting with the world, and self-esteem for children; it is through all they do and say, or lack thereof, that they teach their kids how to be human, for better or for worse.

In the absence of healthy, consistent, and safe upbringings, caregivers, and relationships, many times children will try to find what they are missing in other places, without realizing that often what they are searching for is and will be similar to the feelings from and experiences of the abuse, toxicity, and pain that they experience at home. This is because we seek what is familiar--if all we've experienced since birth is neglect, abandonment, abuse, instability, and chaos of sorts, then this is what we will subconsciously seek out and be drawn to.

And so despite what exciting attractions drew me to the gang life, a horrible misery had always been underneath the glamour. The misery of not having a father or some other proper male role model to mimic, and being unconsciously driven by that same cloud of misery to become subjected to the poisonous influences of criminals, dealers, hustlers, and murderers. The misery of limiting my social circle to those who could only relate to my own sour state, coupled by the misery in being left to rely on, or hold onto, those suffering the same as I. The misery in having every material thing ever hustled, bought or taken, took or lost by the easy come easy go principal customary to street life, and a lack of notion in knowing what true pride in honest hard work felt like. And most critical, the misery in isolation from being held confined,

4

incarcerated in a world of captivity where misery, sorrow, and loneliness walked hand in hand. Gang culture desecrated all of the natural compassion that I held for people as a lad, driving me to mutate as if infected by some abominable virus or germ. Surrounded by a constant circle in the company of others infected with the same disease prevented me from seeing just how debauched I had become.

I've managed to now spend more of life locked inside a cement room called a cell than in the free world. And as life moved on without me, so did the gang. You would think that after all of my loyal devotion to upholding the terror to represent the hood, after all the rage and violence to hold status, someone in the gang would at least respect me enough to care for commissary needs or even my family. At the very least, a greeting card signed by the crew, reminding me of how loved and missed I am. The reality is, after the gang used me up, consumed me, and reduced me to convict, it needed me no more. It went on without me to secure yet another mark to replace me, like plastic utensils discarded after a meal.

My innocence before I was devoured by the gang.

I was seven years old when I first saw the movie "Warriors." It took me on an emotional rollercoaster ride at first because I knew that the Warriors gang would become exiled. Besides being a small group, they were outnumbered, so naturally, I expected them to be swallowed up, falsely accused of a murder that prohibited a global gang truce. But as they ran, they not only fight to survive, they also constructed a plan to clear the gang's name and bring the right culprit to gang justice. The desperation, fear, and determination are what moved me, but even more so, the strength they displayed to resist capture and wrongful execution led me to cheer for the underdog. I learned then that fear could be turned into a source of power to make one strong in times of need and that others who are scared to the point of weakness draw confidence and courage from the strength of one man.

Although I was able to recognize the positive qualities from such a movie and be inspired to persevere in moments of adversity at such a young age, I didn't have a decent father figure or positive male role model to show me how to incorporate what I identified into my individual journey into manhood, and so my personal growth commenced from around the idea of needing a group, crew, or gang to function. I held the misinformed belief that I needed others to bring out my strength and vigor, to rely on or have me to hold them afloat.

So it was no wonder that as fifth grade ended and the sixth grade commenced, I found myself in a circle of friends who favored the color red and drew confidence from one day being a factor in the Mad Swan Blood (MSB) gang, which was extremely difficult to muster because for one, the city of Los Angeles was overpopulated by Crip gangs who truly loved the color blue and outnumbered the boys in red five to one. If they merely had a dream that they were called a "slob," then you would be jumped or likely beat to death.

In these premature stages where being a Blood was just something of lust, I was scared of being known for such, so I would hide my red shoestrings in my pocket until I reached a safe area to duck in a cut to put them on before members of my crew knew. And when it was time to depart, I would do the same in reverse. What influenced and motivated me to take such risks was my first cousin Mr. Freeze, who despite being dark as night, adopted his moniker from our thrill of watching Batman and Robin in the late '70s, early '80s.

Freeze was a glamorous psychopath, trained early on by the older Swan Bloods like Big Gop, Big Regg, Ice Man Morgan, Fly, Dirty Bird, and Shadey, to name a few, to eradicate Crip gangs. This seemed to delight Mr. Freeze because he was infamous for smoking you with a smile. Before my days of foolish risk where I strived to be a Blood, Freeze and I would be in the room with our plastic animal set playing jungle when suddenly one of the older dudes would tap on the bedroom window and say, "Freeze, let's go," and while my heart would beat with fear, Freeze would flash his yellow-stained smile and say "I'll be back," grab the long barrel 38 that fit 357 rounds from the bottom of the upper bunk bed, then hit the door.

Every time he returned he would give me a handful of empty shells and mischievously say, "Flush these down the toilet." Then we'd resume jungle following my loyal

compliance. We never discussed what he actually did which

caused him to return with casings for me to frequently flush,

but I somehow knew it was vicious and violent.

It was through this exchange that I learned not to

disclose the nature of my offense after the dirty deed was done.

Strangely, Mr. Freeze became the first male role model who I

actually had to lace me, and his overprotection was somehow

received as love as he molded many of the premature qualities

and characteristics I came to hold. The overall message I was

taught was to hold your own by being what we called "hard."

And to be regarded as hard, one had to be heartless.

Just before the summer of 1984, I ended up sharing

bunk beds with Mr. Freeze and my oldest brother Nino, in a

two-bedroom apartment being rented by my grandma on 83rd

and Avalon in Los Angeles. It was a two-story building

holding four units on each floor just on the corner of red traffic

lights. Anybody hard or heartless hung out, sold crack cocaine,

or gang banged on the corner of 83rd. My first fight, first

girlfriend, first drug sale, first hundred dollars, first real dream, first arrest, first time getting shot, and first true mistake occurred right on the corner of 83rd and Avalon.

Nino and Freeze trapped in the storm.

Within the first three months of living there, one morning, while carrying out my task of cleaning the room, I came across a chrome 25 pistol with a white handle, secreted inside a pair of the dozens of shoes that lined the closet floor and shelf. I took the pistol outside to show my best chum, K. Rock, then after some time playing with it, enough to figure out the basic mechanical functions, I decided to put it back where I found it. Only I removed the piece from a well-worn white Chuck Taylor Converse shoe belonging to Nino and placed it in a pair of my own less worn Puma sneakers. I figured this way I could rely on some excuse that I misplaced the gun in the wrong shoe when cleaning rather than having to explain flat out to Nino or Freeze that I stole it from the room.

When a couple of days went by without mention or confrontation, I took the gun out because K. Rock and I made plans to buss on some Crips who we knew rode the bus to school on Manchester Ave. The plan was to lay low and wait from an alley directly across from the bus stop, and as soon as they got off the bus faking hard, we'd draw down and shoot, but we had yet to decide which one of us would pull the trigger this first time. K. Rock immediately came to fancy holding the gun in his pocket and pulling it out for effect and attention as a habit, so by the time we ended up in position, he was holding the piece. We stood in the alley's shadow, 3:00 o'clock in the L.A. afternoon, watching as 20 Crips in blue emerged being hard from the RTD. K. Rock froze, so I grabbed the gun from his clammy hand, injected a round into the chamber, emerged from the shadow of the alley, walking to the first lane of traffic in the street, yelled out, "what that Swan like," then opened fire. People fell and scattered until the gun locked from being emptied.

As we ran back towards 83rd, K. Rock yelled with excitement, "We got 'em! We got 'em!" I was overwhelmed with amazement over how I just made a bunch of older hard guys run for their lives from me. That small taste of power gave me a sense of superiority, and I knew that to hold onto this feeling I needed to keep a gun.

Over the next week or two, K. Rock and I made rotated rounds to various bus stops taking turns shooting at anyone we opposed, and in no time Crips recognized us enough to run on sight before we could get off a shot. Word had also traveled back to Nino and Freeze that we were "trying to put in work" for the hood. So, one day after returning from shooting up a bus stop, Nino awaited me in the room demanding, "Where that gun at?" Of course, I tried a plea of ignorance before lying, but each response that didn't produce that gun caused Nino to punch me in the chest repeatedly for about an hour until I finally gave it up. Nino then pulled out a wad of cash, peeled off a 50 bill, gave it to me, and said "Don't ever steal from me. Ask me for whatever you want," then dismissed me to go to Jimbos on 81st and Avalon where K. Rock and I enjoyed double cheeseburgers while laughing over chocolate milkshakes.

As we walked from the burger stand, Freeze turned the corner off Avalon onto 82nd street in his brown 73 Monte Carlo, leaned over to open the passenger door, and with him a scout demanded, "Get in." As K. Rock got in the back and I the

front, Freeze went on a rant. He started off by saying how we

were doing "stupid shit," referring to the shooting in and at

crowds of people, "not knowing what you hitting." Then we

learned that the gun we stole was used by Sike and Pookie to

kill an ice cream man months prior, and the police were

looking hard for that particular murder weapon to seal the

murder charge that they were in Los Padrinos (LP) Juvenile

Hall in Downey, California, fighting. This explanation made it

easy not to hate Nino for the beating he imposed earlier. Just

when I expected to be beaten again by Mr. Freeze, he suddenly

said, "Since ya'll want to buss on crabs, I'ma show ya'll how

to do it right." He then reached under the seat, handed me a 22

long barrel and K. Rock a black 25, then turned up San Pedro

towards Florence Ave, and headed for the heart of the Crip

neighborhood.

Even with loaded guns ready, K. Rock and I were

scared half to death just from being in forbidden areas. Freeze

first turned down a street where we could see Crips in blue

posted in the middle of the block, but as soon as they recognized that brown Monte Carlo, they began running in yards towards the back of houses. As Freeze slammed on the brakes, he turned around and told us to "stay in the car." He jumped out with a 357 magnum and gave chase in pursuit. After what seemed like an eternity, Freeze returned to relieve us from fear well masked behind the pistols held at the ready, and as he reached the Monte Carlo that was irregularly parked as if it were abandoned, he stopped to flirt with a pretty young sister clad in blue who obviously not only knew him but was infatuated by his style. Then just before Freeze got back in the driver's seat to depart he told her, "Tell C. Dog Mr. Freeze came looking for him," and flashed that infamous smile before driving off even deeper into Crip territory.

Soon enough, we came upon a guy on a beach cruiser bike clothed in royal blue. He rode ahead, oblivious to our tailing behind. As Mr. Freeze eased the car next to the rider, I reached out to grab the target's clothing, pulling him towards the door. K. Rock and I emptied pistols at close range into his

17

body before Freeze darted off in haste with the most approving

smile. I learned a few things that day: I learned how to

properly put in work for the gang; I learned how such a violent

act left an effect on me and my conscious; and I learned how to

appeal to Freeze's sense of approval for affection, which was

sparked by the challenge of what I believed was hard or manly.

Freeze would then have K. Rock and me with him

daily, certifying us to the older members as "they ready,"

which then led to Peter Moody and Lil Fats coming to find me

and K. Rock to take us to the other Blood neighborhoods to

fight members our size and age who somehow offended them.

Of course, we had to win to represent Swan right, so we did,

and we became the two youngest members in a gang that was

relatively small yet notorious. We were 13-year old kids in a

jungle of beasts bucking to prove that we were "hard," and

somehow we managed to fit in as if we were prone to being

criminalized.

There was always glamour, even in the most vile of

things we did, that not only drew us deeper into the gang life but also made us quite exceptional as crooks. We now were the ones the older homies came to get to put in work, and because of the loyalty we demonstrated on 83rd Street, we caught the interest of Nate. Nate was a college boy who lived just off the corner of Towne Ave on 83rd, who befriended a schoolmate whose family had tons of cocaine. This made Nate an East Side King Pen.

Posted out front Grandma's sitting on Scar's legendary

Fleetwood, a gift from Nate, 1985.

Since as early as 1984, everybody who lived on 83rd or represented its values, Nate had under structure selling crack cocaine in the most organized fashion. Certain houses or apartments he rented were turned into what is called a "spot." For K. Rock and me, Nate insisted that we return to finish school if we intended on working, and if we missed a day of school we couldn't work in the spot. Working in the spot meant starter jackets, hats, and sportswear from Sports Spectacular in downtown LA, Levi jeans, Corduroys, Dickies, Litegere, and Pumas from Chicagos off Western on Vermont, and accessories from the Fox or Baldwin Hill malls, so of course, we fell into the structure implemented by Nate. Therefore, we were in school at South Park Elementary doing 6th-grade class with Mrs. Belcher from 8:00 a.m. to 2:15 p.m., then from about 4:00 p.m. until 6:00 a.m., we were in the spot selling crack.

School was interesting enough because of the relationship I had with Mrs. Belcher who was infamous for being a no-nonsense teacher. Initially, about three times during the first week we met she would tell me, "John, we're going to the hospital for me to get my leg cut off and you to get my foot

out yo ass," which caused everybody to laugh except me since

I was always secretly scared of that wild look in Mrs. Belcher

eyes when she was mad. I learned quickly that Mrs. Belcher

liked me because despite my mischief and misdeeds in school,

we never made it to the hospital. Within two months, I would

arrive at school an hour or so early to help set up the

classroom, reorganize the cash made in the spot, and run to

Wenchels's to grab a coffee and jelly donut for Mrs. Belcher. I

listened to her vent about her marriage and loaned her money,

which she always paid back.

Working in the spot was endless excitement and

adventure because although one didn't always know what to

expect, one always knew to expect something, and being ready

for anything is what drove the excitement. The spots all had

basic furniture: a couch, a living room as well as kitchen

tables, and of course, beds. There was a giant metal bowl on

every living room table which held liquid acid in the event that

the police raided. If the spot was raided, we were instructed to make sure all the drugs were in the bowl before the door broke down. Fortunately, we never were raided so we never bothered or tested the acid.

There were, however, an endless stream of characters addicted to the crack rock, who used vast manipulation or lies (which we called game), schemes, and plays in order to smoke for free. In those days, spots were equipped with bars on the windows and doors, and every door or window would have a hole cut into it just big enough to exchange cash and drugs without having to open the door. The minimum purchase was a quarter rock for $25--there were no $5, $10, or even $20 rocks.

K. Rock and I didn't quite like the system of serving through the hole in the door, so we developed our own. When customers came knockin', he would let them inside, and I would hide behind the entrance door with a pistol ready to shoot. People would always initially assume, because we were so small, that there was someone else they would be dealing with until we demonstrated that take-charge behavior, such as emerging from behind the door, gun out, demanding they "sit down, put the money on the table, and don't put your hands in your pocket." Then upon departure, we insisted that they "don't walk out with that in your hand, put it in your mouth." There were many times when there were 15 to 20 customers in the spot at one time, and we would hold them all hostage until everyone had been served and they could all leave together. I learned crowd control and how important it was for people to take you seriously. I also learned that in order for people to take you seriously, you had to be prepared to react seriously.

There was a time when a bunch of people came to score and included in the bunch was James, the father of one of my homeboys who had yet to blossom into the thug life. Well, James was impatient after buying his crack one night and insisted that I open the door so he could leave. At James' demand, I sensed others eager to follow suit so I pointed the 22 pistol and shot twice, striking James in the chest and shoulder yelling, "don't come in here telling me how to run my spot." Then at gunpoint, with one hand over his chest to thwart the flow of blood, I made him sit down until everyone was done. A few hours later, a guy and two women came to cop (buy) some crack. One of the women insisted she be allowed to "taste" the crack before paying for it and in her "taste" she switched the crack rock for some fake rock she had hidden in her lying mouth. This prompted both K. Rock and I to draw pistols and commence whipping each of them sporadically, chasing them around and tearing up the spot for the thrill of getting a hit in. We didn't act to retrieve the product, we were too caught up in the joy of the attack, and in the end, we both ended up beating the guy unconscious, then accused him of faking that before allowing them to leave, holding their bloody head and faces in their sweaty palms.

From working in the spot I learned to hold one against their will and to force them to comply with whatever I said. I also learned the flavor of captor, close torture, and of course, violence, which led me to believe and actually feel hard from victimizing others. It seemed as though for every person I succeeded in harming, I took something from them that made me more and more powerful. Then the craving for more of that feeling consumed me, and erupting to violence in any situation became desired.

Within an hour following the second incident, Nate sent one of his henchmen, my older homie Master Blaster, to remove us from the spot and bring us to him. We were expecting a scolding, but Nate walked us to H & H Cafe on Avalon and 82nd Street for a pork chop dinner with sweet potato pie. The whole time he commended us for protecting the product as well as sending a clear message about the seriousness of business, especially to those who would think to rob us.

Our actions led to us receiving a promotion from working in the spot to patrol. Patrol came with the responsibility of guarding each of Nate's spots, collecting cash from each spot, and replenishing the spots with cocaine. If someone pulled shenanigans at any one of the spots, we would be given their name and identity, and while on patrol, track them down while hiding out in one of the many base houses throughout the east side of South-Central. The last thing

26

anyone wanted or needed was to be on our hitlist because aside from having the alliance of many addicts who held houses or apartments that users relied on to free base in comfort or solitude, we had become infamous for enjoying the thrill of terrorizing and not caring about the risk or consequence.

Nate paid us both two hundred dollars a week for patrol duties and supplied various cars rented from users for us to get around in order to be effective. Initially, neither of us knew how to drive and the first time we commenced patrol, he simply told us what was expected and needed, pointed to the vehicle we'd be using, then handed us the keys. We learned to drive by getting in the car and taking turns with the seat let all the way up, sitting on a pillow or two as we navigated through the streets of Los Angeles, running up on street curbs when turning corners, side sweeping parked cars, overheating engines, even crashing then jumping out abandoning our transportation until we figured it all out. It took about two to three months and the destruction of about four to six cars before we mastered the art of driving. The manner in which we

27

were tasked with a responsibility, then left to figure out how to best handle or carry it out gave us the sense of belonging and the feeling of being respected as men. Having a crew to support and defend us whether right or wrong, and often call upon us in need of what service or skill we had to offer made us feel needed, appreciated, and loved, and to hold on to such feeling we held a sick sense of pride in loyalty to the street life and to each other.

The fact that Nate had implemented school attendance in the structure gave us the belief that we weren't as bad as we actually were; in fact, we believed that things like being a snitch, a buster, an addict, scared, or broke, were the type of things that would render us bad or no good. If we didn't stay fresh, move product, or react quick to violence, we believed we lost or had no respect, and if we sold poor quality cocaine, ran out of such, was forced to walk around due to having no car, didn't have money saved up, didn't shoot when necessary, denounced membership in the gang or became known as "in love" or willing to splurge on a female, we were ridiculed to shame, clowned, and deprived of being taken seriously throughout the neighborhood.

To avoid such things, we perfected the image of being hard, which became a normal way of life. At school, I confided in Mrs. Belcher regularly as if she were my priest; with every sin or foul deed I shared with her, she would often give me a scowl look in a twisted way of concern, then say things like, "Boy where is yo damn daddy?,"

"You better always keep yo ass in school," or

"You goin' give yo momma a heart attack boy."

Mrs. Belcher didn't want us to bring our guns into the class or school, so the moment I reached her classroom before school fully commenced, she would give me the keys to her dark brown four-door Mercedes, and I'd sneak down to stash the pistols in her trunk or under the passenger's front seat. Then after school, I'd enjoy carrying her matching Italian case as I walked her to her car for the day and retrieved the weapons. We always kept a g-ride, parked a block or two from school under the radar. Monday through Thursday, Mrs.

Belcher taught the class with a unique lesson of her own,

which was always educational, intense, and fun. Stragglers or

those who didn't belong roaming the hall well knew not to

disrupt Mrs. Belcher's class. At the end of the school week, she

had a personal holiday called "Thank God it's Friday," where

she only taught for the first hour or two then let me leave to

buy the whole class donuts, candy, hamburgers with fries and

sodas, and we'd eat and clown all day over "yo momma

jokes." But after school, it was back on patrol.

K. Rock and I were trained to always buy guns

whenever addicts came up with them, and as a collective, we

held an arsenal of an array of weapons such as pistols and

rifles. Yet in secret, K. Rock and I were scared to shoot any

caliber above a 25 because of the monstrous kick in the recoil,

and despite the fact that we had already grown too accustomed

to unloading at close range on those we regarded as enemies,

we remained amazed in fear by the loud boom noise 38's,

357's and 45's made when shot, and especially by the licks of

flame that came from the barrels as slugs emerged. After

learning that we had acquired a fairly new sawed-off 12 gauge pump, Peter Moody and Lil Fats pulled up on 83rd early one morning in that dark blue 1965 Chevy with a 22 carbine rifle insisting that we trade, and of course we happily agreed. The next day, however, Lil Fats blew Peter's brains out of his head with that same 12 gauge by accident while patrolling the neighborhood by Crips who knew that blue Chevy. While Peter was driving up Towne Ave, Crips had opened fire with a pistol, striking Peter somewhere in the left side of the face, and as Lil Fats tried to ward off the assassins by aiming the 12 gauge in the direction of the shooter, he blew off the right side of Peter's forehead, causing the Chevy to crash in halt into Fremont High School gate on 78th and Towne.

K. Rock and I had heard of homies like Big Chuck, Elvis, Froot Loop, Big Fats, Ice Man Morgan, Black Bird, Monsta John, and Big Bop, to name a few, who had been shot and killed by Crips for the hood, but this was the first homie we actually knew, did dirt with, and had an abundance of fun with who had died, and the fact that it was a gun that came from us that was used to end his life made Peter's death more personal. We didn't blame the Crips or Lil Fats, we blamed ourselves, but hid behind the vow of revenge in Peter's memory. From this experience, I learned the weight of guilt as it hammered at my heart, and I learned how to suppress that feeling of guilt behind the violence I believed avenged my dead homie.

Struck and left with guilt's burden, which we were unable to process or even address, K. Rock and I were brought even closer. The only thing we didn't do as one was take a shit together, and just like with the gang, we overprotected each other by being violent.

Outside of school, K. Rock and I had no friends or even girlfriends our own age. Boke, who was a year older than us, was the youngest friend we had and yet was considered an old man at 15 because since Boke was in diapers, the older homeboys raised him. Boke killed his first Crip at the age of nine, witnessed Big Fats killed right next to him by Crips while selling weed on San Pedro and 84th Street when he was 12, and had also survived being blasted by Crips with a 12 gauge close range, so he always held a lot of anger. What Boke had already endured, K.Rock and I were new in experiencing, so it is no surprise that we leaned on Boke in wake of Peter's death. Despite the tragic horrors, we kept patrol to keep them spots jumpin' for Nate because despite the traumatic events and in light thereof, if you don't work you can't eat, and the California prime motto is and always was "money talk and bullshit walk."

Although I had passed challenges required to be accepted into the gang, I had yet to be tested in a way where I was at risk of losing what I valued most next to life itself--my freedom. The street life and gang come with a series of cycles which serve as some sort of test in determining the type of criminal one is, and at some point, that criminal will be held to answer for some crime or pay the piper, as some say. Mine came unexpectedly one morning in the summer of 1985, when three teenage kids clad in blue came up 83rd from Central Ave to Avalon hoping to score a couple of ounces of crack. I asked them, "Where ya'll from?" and they claimed a Crip gang from

Watts. I then asked, "Ya'll know where ya'll at?" and of course they did, but they figured since they came to do business and were desperate enough to risk coming on 83rd, that it would be worth it. I immediately led them into Apartment 1 at 8229 South Avalon, right next to my grandma's apartment where we all lived. Then I went next door to alert my big homie and Mr. Freeze's partner in crime, Tray Doose, who was about five years older than me.

Tray Doose, Hyde and Freeze in glimpse of betta dayz.

Tray Doose smiled then quickly instructed that I go back next door to the spot to engage the three as a stall tactic. He never said his intention, but after a few minutes of stalling, Tray Doose came through one of the bedroom windows into the living room with a 38 pistol in hand to announce in a calm yet rugged tone, "this is a robbery." With one hand on the gun pointed at each face, the other hand began to quickly remove wads of cash from their pockets, stuffing the take into his own.

When Tray Doose reached the third victim, he decided to try to run to avoid giving up his cash but Tray Doose immediately shot him through the torso twice and he fell onto the floor just in front of the door. The shots sounded as loud as thunder, and I thought about how it would sound to the neighbors since this unit was empty from in between tenants.

I quickly came back to reality and noticed how the teenage boy wasn't resisting as Tray Doose calmly walked over to empty his pockets and how his two homies stood still as day paralyzed by fear. I doted over the performance Tray Doose displayed as if he had a power I too wanted to relish and rain on others. Tray Doose then opened the front door, looked outside, and told the two survivors to stand on each side of the punctured kid to help him up and leave. We stood on the corner watching as the three went back up 83rd toward Central Ave until we couldn't see them anymore, then went into the room where Tray Doose split the three grand he had with me and Freeze before disappearing.

Two weeks later, on one summer morning, as I walked out the door fresh, a sheriff's car was parked at the curb waiting for me. Two deputies emerged from the vehicle and detained me, as they raced another sheriff's car to the station in which Tray Doose was being held handcuffed in the back. Along the way, I was able to see and read the big homie eyes and gather from the constant shaking of his head "no" that I had to keep my mouth shut and lips sealed when the interrogation came. I had already decided to deny knowing the people shot and robbed and deny any knowledge of a robber or robbery. The deputy then reiterated the events and told me if Tray Doose made me or forced my participation that I could be a witness and they'd call my mom to pick me up with the understanding that I had to appear as a witness. I told the deputy again that I knew nothing of a robbery or a shooting, and especially could not help them find the weapon that Tray Doose supposedly used. They pressed me to crack while other deputies went to search Tray Doose and my rooms at our homes, hoping to find the gun or that I would cave and turn on Tray Doose but I didn't. I ended up in LP Unit X-Y which was for juveniles 13 and under, while Tray Doose went to unit E-F which was for adult teenagers who gang banged with force.

As soon as I walked in and saw the other kids in the X-Y unit of the juvenile prison, they hit me with, "Where you from?" and my reply of, "Mad Swan Blood" got a lot of them riled up, so much so that as soon as I was assigned my one-man room where I only had time to make up the steel bed, a tall dark-skinned athletic kid, obviously older and bigger than me, walked inside my room, closed the door, stood facing me with one foot leaned against the wall, then said with contempt, "What that Hoover Crip like cuzz, fuck slobbs."

To which I replied, "Fool this Swan, fuck crabs." As I stood from the bed to square off with this guy, we began to fight. He used his height and weight to hold my arms so that I couldn't swing to shut me down as I repeated, "Let me go punk so I can show you what that Swan like," constantly maneuvering in an effort to free myself from his clench. In his last attempt, the guy released his hold to throw a punch while dashing for the door to exit the room but I was quick and already was punching at his face relentlessly, so in the midst of his fleeing, he smacked his face on the room door and took shots from my fists as he left.

Afterward, I got in trouble for being outside my room in the hall all riled up. The people supervising the unit wrote me up and made the threat of sending me to "the box," which I learned later is disciplinary isolation for disruptive juveniles. The only contact one had in the box was meals and medication for a set period of seven up to 30 days. I recognized that I could feel safer in the box than in the unit, so naturally, I would come to spend most of the 90-120 day sentence in the box.

When I was on the unit, I felt like if I didn't find a target to attack in violence, then I would become another's target. So the way to avoid being hunted, one had to hunt, and so I became the hunter, and the only escape from either was in the box.

The guy who came into my room turned out to be T.Bone from 107 Hoover. We not only fought a time or two again under other circumstances, but his homies Tank and Lil Shadey from 74 Hoover also became involved. Apparently, T.Bone was a young rider on the rise, infamous for winning more than a few fights in the unit, but the bruises on his face after leaving my room caused mainly by the door diminished his reputation, which made little ole me appear hard, and that meant an endless battle with almost every Crip in the unit. The only refugee was being sent to the box.

My behavior on the unit caught the attention of Lil Baldey from 83 Hoover who was a well-known OG housed on E-F with Tray Doose. Lil Baldey and I were in the same class in juvenile hall school, and every day he would harass me saying because his lil homies T.Bone, Tank, and Lil Shadey couldn't "handle me," that he had some lil homies housed on unit G-H (which is where graduates from unit X-Y go when over 13), who were gonna show me "what that Hoover was like." Lil Baldey would always mention to me how I was lucky to be so small, otherwise, he'd get me himself. Fortunately, I never had to meet none of his lil homies from G-H, and although I responded like I was ready and hard, I was scared every day which also made my frequent trips to the box more enjoyable.

Tray Doose and I would only see each other in court at the Juvenile Justice Center (JJC) on Central Ave, where the public defender assigned to represent me kept telling me, "You can go home today if you tell the court that your co-defendant did everything without you knowing." But I was scared to talk and wasn't the only one. As it turns out, although the victims detailed to the sheriff's what had occurred, they had apparently already made it clear that they would not and could not testify in open court. So after three non-appearances at the preliminary hearing, the judge was forced to dismiss the case.

I had no idea that this would be the most significant moment in my life--having my freedom restored as a reward for my silence--which sold the bogus idea and concept of a gang, as I believed loyalty to my homies, which made up the gang, was my primary duty and requirement aside from working the spot. I had been given and taken the final test, and I didn't come close to snitching on Tray Doose.

To the homies I was solid, but the truth is, had I flipped on Tray Doose, I may have gotten beaten and exiled, but more so, the homies would've known I had catted and would likely tell again, spill the beans or snitch, and with such stigma, I would never become a factor in gang life. You have to understand that at twelve years of age, with no male guidance other than from crooks, gang banging was not just the most exciting thing going, but the most common pathway carved out for misguided and many fatherless youth--at least to a naive kid.

When my mom came to collect me from LP, I was so relieved, and she was so excited that I "beat the case." I wasn't scolded or lectured at all--my mom didn't even talk to me about what happened. In fact, my mother dropped me off on 83rd, took some cash I gifted her for gas, and grateful for freedom, asked for a kiss on the cheek, then went up Avalon on 88th Place to go home to an apartment complex called the Avalon Gardens. The Avalon Gardens were in Crip territory and the Crips who lived there hated me, feared Mr. Freeze, and vowed to kill Nino since my mom moved into their projects around 1983.

The first thing I noticed when I got back on the corner of my block was that Apartment 1, where we did the crime, was occupied. There was a bright red 1973 Chevy Blazer with a black strip around the body, equipped with a leather detachable top parked directly out front of our spot, Apartment 2. It was a gift to Nino from Nate for his loyal service and hard work. This blazer came with a racing engine, so it was faster than a New York minute with sounds loud like a disco show.

The police had come with the batter ram to take the doors off of the hinges at the spots, so Nate turned most of the spots into safe houses for storage. In my short absence, my big homie Scar, who was previously smoked out on crack, had taken a dope case for Nate, and in exchange, Nate cleaned him up to where Scar was now selling kilos. Nate even gave him the legendary yellow Fleetwood, which one could also find parked on 83rd with the Blazer since Scar lived directly upstairs from us in the apartments.

While I was incarcerated, K. Rock had fallen under the structure of Scar and became a baby baller since his primary focus was working a spot 24/7 with Scar. But my return promoted K. Rock to resume where we had left off, and the balance between banging for the hood and working the spot became a challenge because gang banging was in high function and the murder rate stayed on the rise. My neighborhood was surrounded by and in the middle of various Crip gangs--it was small, with only a few blocks as with the 89 neighborhood family. The gang's survival depended on a murderous terror, of which we all did well, and the many unfortunate casualties

alongside those slewn in retaliation were the motivational fuel

that also haunted the consciousness of us all. Yet, we had the

image of being hard and heartless to hide behind.

Within two weeks of being home, my eleven-year-old

cousin Angel told me her best friend Deserray, A.K.A. Snoopy,

not only liked me but had chosen me to be her man.

My cousin -- a true angel whose light shines on.

Snoopy was almost 14 years old, a year younger than me, and like me, she lived making her own choices unless someone dared stop us. Initially, she told me how a lot of my homies had been trying to get her open, especially K. Rock, who frightened her. Apparently, Angel matched us long before I would win my case and Snoopy waited. She was living next door with her Samoan single mother and her six-year-old sister who were both half Black. Come to find out Snoopy resented her mother for being sexually abused by a dude her mom had invited to come live in their home.

I shared a similar relation where, for as long as I can remember, my mother's best friend Patricia Jones, A.K.A. Pat, sexually exploited and abused me whenever she babysat or lived with us until I was about nine years old, but I didn't describe it to Snoopy as abuse nor as some complaint. In fact, I had always considered it as "Pat turned me out," as if it were some noble deed installed, but having this in common solidified our union at a fast pace.

Within a month, I trusted her to hold and hide money, guns, and cocaine in her room, where I frequently visited by crawling through the same bedroom window that Tray Doose had used to rob the three teenage Crips months prior.

Although Snoopy and I didn't even have pubic hairs, we were entwined in sexual proclivities intended only for adults. Somehow we believe we needed the engagement, as much as we needed to soothe each other in pleasures of the flesh. But despite the bond I shared with Snoopy, she always knew that I put the gang before her, perhaps even wise enough to know back then that I was fool enough to even put the gang before me. Whether I knew it or not is of no matter, for in the overall scheme of things, the gang consumes and affects every aspect of one's life as there is no "part-time" to banging. When one's foe catches you with loved ones in family mode, they still resort to violence to show offense and that is a sure way to openly invite madness to traumatize loved ones.

The gang kept high demand on Swans needed to represent its blood, and blood did spill in vengeance, through retaliation, and by innocence. Gang banging was still fresh in '85 and although many Blood and Crip gangs thrived throughout South Los Angeles, none had quite conquered the other; all the while, they were misled by the trivial notion that they actually could, so each day we lived to penetrate another's neighborhood with violence so ferocious that weaker gangs would eventually fade. The Swans were at war with so many Crip gangs individually that not a day went by where some rival didn't do a walk or drive-by shooting. There were bullet holes inside and out of our apartment building. Even the cars that parked regularly were peppered with holes from slugs meant for one of us.

One morning, after leaving through the window of Snoopy's bedroom at about 5:00 a.m., I went home next door to get fresh, intending on being out early since there was a regular clientele on weekdays who liked to score crack rock en route to work. As I was out sitting on the hood of Scar's Fleetwood, flamed up (clad in red clothing head to toe), 22 pistol in pocket, with a handful of cocaine rocks, a police car rode by without stopping, so out of caution, I quickly ran to put the pistol under the couch in the house then went back on post. I had already learned how to talk with crack rocks in my mouth, so I felt safe for the moment.

However, not ten minutes after I returned to sit on the Fleetwood, a brown Pinto turned off Avalon onto 83rd, where the passenger held a 38 and pointed as the car halted before me. I immediately thought of my gun under the couch as I sprung off the hood, turned my back to the shooter, and began running toward the house. Shots rang out, one hitting me in the right thigh before going straight through my bone, knocking me down. I managed to crawl behind the Fleetwood to shield myself just in time to see my big homie T.Bone emerge from one of the apartments upstairs with a chrome 357 magnum shooting slugs.

As the Pinto dashed off, T.Bone was reloading as Mr. Freeze turned the corner with Tray Doose in grandma's legendary Delta 88, saw me on the ground, looked ahead at the fleeing car, then gave chase, rubber burning. It wasn't until I was on a gurney about to be placed in the ambulance on the way to Martin Luther King Jr. Hospital in Watts that I remembered I still had the crack in my hand secured by a fist. I gave it to my older homie Roll Out, who was the big brother of Big Noon, then told him I had more rocks on the turntable in the room and asked him to hold it. He would smoke up what I trust he'd hold while I had surgery on my leg, flirting with a sister assigned as one of my nurses who couldn't stop playing in my jerry curls, to disconnect me mentally from the pain which felt like burning heat that numbed my feet.

My mom showed up like she always did for me, to take me home, but this time she asked if I wanted to "go back on 83rd" as if to inquire whether getting shot was enough to deter me from the gang while at the same time knowing already that I'd insist on being back on the block. I had her drop me off on Avalon, gave her a kiss, some cash, then hopped on my crutches around the corner into the room as my homegirls Deb, Tammy, Keshia Lowe, and Daniel doted in sympathy by my wound. Since Roll Out had already been demoted by Nate, he became my personal bodyguard tasked with ensuring my safety until I could walk, only he didn't pack or shoot guns so I convinced my grandma that crutches would work best for her around the apartment and her wheelchair would be fine for me to go out with. While Roll Out pushed me around up and down Avalon, where I sold crack and shot at passing cars throughout the day and night, in the 'wee wee's,' Snoopy would exit her room window to hang out and play, but even that was dependent upon the level of wrath the gang war held because although 83rd between Stanford and San Pedro was a gold mine for cocaine dealers, everybody hated Swans. So if some car wasn't passing by doing what some East Coast Crips called "duck huntin," some murderer like Mr. Freeze would calmly walk close enough to do what I came to call "take yo picture," to mysteriously vanish after leaving one or more person disfigured in execution from gunshots.

One couldn't sell crack or even hang without heat or a pistol, and people kept coming by looking to slaughter you. To survive this life, one had to like or even live gunfighting. We never recognized a leader of the gang; recognition, respect, influence, control, and fear only came to Swans who put in work with the gun and were measured by how often one left crime scenes. The whole point in gang banging was to kill those believed to be a foe, so if you weren't killing then you weren't banging, and if you didn't bang then you had no real say so, position, or protection over or from those regarded as killers.

Growing both impatient with healing and disgusted with Rollout smoking my crack and not wanting to not rely on him made me try to walk to get around prematurely. I didn't tell anyone how he did me, neither did I ever confront him or receive some apology. I just insisted one day that I didn't need his help and commenced hopping around as if I could walk, ignoring the pain. Gang banging held such an appeal that I felt lonely and left out hearing K. Rock and other homies speak of adventures that either occurred or were to come. Feeling like I was missing something in the streets gave me the daring idea to get in the black 69 Chevy that K. Rock and I had purchased and split the cost of $400 from the OG homie Dimp from Bounty Hunters to patrol the neighborhood, pistol in lap, eager to be seen or regarded as back on the prowl defending the gang. I was accustomed to driving using my right foot so the injury compelled me to experiment with the left instead.

While getting gas at the station on Manchester and San Pedro Ave, I saw rival Crips at Tom's Burgers across the street. Apparently, they didn't react to me since I wasn't clad in red, and as I departed up Manchester Ave toward Main Street, only to make a u-turn that caused the other drivers' horns to blow. They still weren't concerned with me. I turned into Tom's driveway as if to park in the customer section only to stop after clearing the driveway. I got out, hopped toward the counter to order, then opened fire as four Crips awaited their food. They caught on, but much too late. Two shots with the perfect aim at each rival's face and head was the mission, but I had to settle on the fourth victim's torso as he fled out of range of the hollow points coming from the nine-shot 22.

I noticed the Mexicans working Tom's Stand and Grill staring at me with wide eyes, mouths open, before I saw the black and white police car making a right off Manchester onto San Pedro in order to access the scene by coming through the gas station next door. In a panic, I hopped back to the Chevy, swerved through the back of Tom's, just in time to pass right by the police as I gunned the engine across San Pedro up Manchester then onto Towne Ave, desperate to make it back to 83rd. But as I rounded the corner, the gas pedal got stuck--before I could straighten the wheel, I crashed into the mechanic shop back gate. I immediately jumped out the passenger side with the pistol and ran like hell up the alley, down another, and back up again until I realized how badly my leg hurt. I had a brief thought to throw the gun then surrender, but I thought of LP and how it smelled, and T.Bone, so I resumed running until I reached my block where I went to the room, changed clothes, and laid down in relief before laughing.

Mr. Freeze came in sometime later and with that devilish smile of approval, simply asked, "What you done did?" This was the first mission I put down solo, and I learned quickly that this was the type of thing that commanded respect, praise, and attention from other members of the gang. I held water on the case with Tray Doose, took a bullet, and before healed, put down my first solo mission. Now the whole neighborhood was saying I was "crazy like Freeze," which was like a Nobel prize that Freeze took credit for by reiterating, "I created you."

The recognition and acceptance are what made me feel loved, but K. Rock threatened to tarnish that by wanting to fight me because I "fucked off the car" by wreck and impound. Even as I reimbursed his two hundred dollars, he still insisted we fight so we did, and I lost for lack of balance. But somehow losing made me even more popular, because homeboys and girls from all over came to 83rd to greet, smoke weed, drink, and feed me. K. Rock and I stopped hanging daily like we did, and Snoopy would watch from a window in their living room until I found time to engage her. In all the attention and praise, I forgot about her or that she lived next door until I saw her.

Her mother hated me so it was easy, but Snoopy was dedicated and beyond patient, so in the wee wee's, I would always find my way back to her bed and arms, and though I had become drunk with fame, she never refused to hold my cocaine or guns and never stole or took the money.

Somehow, after my first solo mission and fight with K. Rock, the soreness in my leg subsided, and I was healed and ready for full duty. One afternoon, Nate came walking up 83rd with his chow and told me to come to H & H Cafe with him for lunch, which was always his treat. As we ate, he told me I would be getting my own sack from now on through Scar, but I was only to turn over my count to him personally. Ounces of cocaine then were $1,500 whole, but selling rocks made $2,500 to $2,700. Nate said to expect two ounces from Scar from which I would only owe him $2,500. Then he said what he was famous for, which was, "Don't fuck me."

A couple of days later, Scar gave me a paper bag with only an ounce, and when I demanded the other ounce Scar claimed, "That's all he gave me for you." So I started marching up 83rd towards Nate's house to confront him about "fuckin'

me," when Scar then gave me the other ounce of cocaine,

laughed, and said he was, "only making sure I was ready for

this responsibility."

This was yet another significant moment I had yet to

grasp. Nate giving me my own cocaine to sell on my own

without a spot or supervision meant that I had become certified

in the streets as fully able to hold my own and that I did

because I was never short and didn't have Nate waiting two to

three weeks for his money like some. With K. Rock's hussle

devoted to Scar, I hooked up with Boke, and we'd be up all

night, paying some addict on crack to drive us around to

different spots where cocaine was smoked to hustle, and when

it was time to put in work, we'd have the driver park around

the block or up the street as we walked to the target prey,

threatening to shoot the driver if, after running back to where

we instructed they wait, they weren't there when we came.

One morning, as if nothing happened, I came outside to

find K. Rock cutting up crack cocaine with a razor on the trunk of grandma's Delta 88, and we reconnected like long-lost pals. Apparently, he and Scar had some fallout over money, and K. Rock was convinced that he could do better on his own. Resuming this friendship would turn out to be a critical mistake on my part because K. Rock was infamous for being an instigator with a temper, and the love we all held for him made us vulnerable to be influenced by his frequent tantrums.

As we resumed our devotion to the gang, we also became even more protective of each other, so much so that Snoopy voiced the opinion that I was making a mistake going back to hang with K. Rock, which led us to our first fight. I ended up slapping her for what I called "speaking bad on the homie," but in reality, she was only trying to warn me about what she knew was true. However, I was too under the influence of the gang culture to listen or realize that *a real man is prone to protect, honor, and respect women, and that includes listening to her voice of reason and always keeping her safe from harm, even my own.*

One evening, Poo Bear and Dray pulled up on 83rd in a g-ride asking me if they could borrow some guns to do a mission on some kitchen Crips who were pretending to be too hard. The plan initially was for all of us to do the mission then drink and smoke weed at one of Poobear's lady friends' spots. K. Rock was beyond excited as he insisted that I "get the heat from that bitch," and when I went to Snoopy's window like always and moved the curtain, she had her red rag on to tie her long silky black hair as she lay prone on her bed, legs bent up crossed at the ankles, facing away from the window, talking on the phone while counting cash I had checked in. As I called her name, she jumped up happy to see me, smiling since I had been quite affectionate in my remorse since slapping her weeks prior, but when I said "give me both the rifles, all three pistols and all them extra bullets," her smile turned into a worried expression as she asked, "What you 'finna do?"

When I briefly told her, she said she had a bad feeling and didn't want me to go, so I demanded she "give me my shit," to which she agreed, then went to turn off the light and left her room. About five minutes later she returned claiming that her mother found the guns and took them, then begged me to come inside to bed, which angered me even more because I knew she was lying, and as we argued K. Rock came weighing in calling her a bitch, which made me defend her by yelling, "I told you don't talk to her like that," close to punching him in the mouth.

I didn't care that he called her a bitch--I just didn't want him to say it directly to her and especially in front of me, so as he and I argued, Poo Bear and Dray drove off which sent K. Rock mad on a rant, and as soon as he tried to say, "You let this bitch fuck off the mission," I attacked him at bitch, dominating the fight as if I were out to make up for the previous loss. When done, I turned to Snoopy and said "give me all my shit before I kick your door in and kill yo momma." She quickly went to retrieve the weapons and gave them to me then stood with her arms crossed, and when I repeated, "all my shit," she handed me the cash and cocaine in two shoe boxes. She cried a lake of tears as I went home.

A couple of hours later, K. Rock came knocking on my room window asking why I had left him out there alone like he was confused, and yet again we resumed our friendship as if nothing happened. This time he half apologized for calling Snoopy a bitch and I admitted that she did ruin the mission and deserved to be punished. Sad to say, but our primary concern was that we would look like we punked out on the mission and would look scary to the gang we had already proven to be down for.

So, initially I had decided to punish Snoopy by taking her on a mission and make her shoot someone, but then K. Rock suggested if we were caught by police she was sure to snitch, so it would be better to make her have sex with him instead. At first, I frowned my face because it sounded sick, but then I thought since I have all my shit I was done with her, and she hated and feared K. Rock so that would teach her a cold lesson about getting in Swan business. As soon as I agreed, K. Rock insisted I put it on Swan to commit, knowing that whenever a member made a vow on the gang, there was no welching otherwise one would be regarded as "blowing up the hood" and subject to some form of discipline at gang gatherings or meetings.

Later that night in the early wee wee's of the morning, I couldn't sleep, so I went to Snoopy's window where I heard her crying, and when she realized it was me, she opened the window to let me in as she admitted being wrong for getting in hood business and would never do so again. Then after passionate sex, I told her of the position I got myself in and how I offered her up to K. Rock as punishment, and though I now regretted it, I couldn't pull out. She said she'd do anything except that with him and how she always knew that was what he always wanted. Then she said as long as I was there and we stayed a couple she would do it.

But that morning as K. Rock showed up like the reaper ready to collect his soul, Snoopy wanted to back out. But I took her hand as I led her to Robert Payton's spot on 82nd to rent a room in his plush smokehouse, encouraging her to goin' get it over with. I wouldn't let him force her or be violent but I forced her by holding her hostage in that room, saying she couldn't leave until she did what we came to do. She would start undressing, then put on her clothes as she hugged me, begging me not to make her do it. I sat on the dresser pushing her away over and over again while K. Rock laid naked on the bed grinning like a fat cat until Snoopy finally gave in and had sex with him, crying the whole time as I vowed to myself to never hurt or let her be hurt again. We went into that room around 8:00 o'clock that morning, but as we departed huddled together, it was around 7 in the evening and dark outside -- yet it only took K. Rock five minutes to finish.

As soon as we hit 83rd, Lil Snow came running up to us saying that Snoopy's mother had been in distress trying to find her and the police had been in her apartment for about an hour now. Snoopy told me not to trip, that she'd take care of it, kissed me then ran home. When we saw her, her mom, and sister get into the police car and drive away, we knew something was wrong. Snoopy's payback to K. Rock was exposing what he did, only she lied saying that I rescued her, so now the police were leaving cards at my house asking me to help with some investigation, but Snoopy's mother had already painted me evil, so I knew it was all a set up and avoided going home.

When her family left that night with the police, they never returned, but Snoopy would call Angel to get in touch with me, and I'd often sneak off to Carson, California where they lived so that I could be with and take care of her. After about four or five months, the police caught me on 83rd and caught K. Rock a few days later, then charged us with "lewd act with a child under 14" despite the fact that we were 13 when the act occurred, yet we had turned 14 by the time we were arrested.

Snoopy refused to testify, so the court allowed her mom to, and everything she said was about me killing people, selling dope, and gang banging, all of which I wasn't charged with. My lawyer established Snoopy was my girlfriend and we were sexually involved for months, so I had no reason to force her into sex. After we were bound over for trial, the D.A. told me that he knew Snoopy would lie to protect me and when he forced her to the stand at trial and she lied under oath, that he would charge her with perjury, and if I ever cared for her I wouldn't put her through that. So I took a deal on a guilt plea for a 90-day observation in California Youth Authority followed by eight to 12 months in long-term Camp Vernon Kilpatrick in Malibu, California, while K. Rock got six months in short-term Camp Scott and was back on 83rd in five months flat.

Snoopy would write to me often in Kilpatrick where I did 13 to 14 months, reassuring me that she'd wait for me, forgave me, and still loved me. She would keep me updated on the gang, like when Nate got robbed and killed in 1986 and when my grandma died soon after.

Bitter sweet remembrance of a chum. Rest in Peace, Nate.

Despite Snoopy's devotion and undying love, all I loved and cared about at that point in time was the damn gang and proving to be hard as one of its young soldiers. So naturally, many of my days in camp were spent in dispute with Moon and Lil Devil from Front hood and Ice Man from Harlem Crip, while banging the 'B' with Twin, Brown Eyes, and Rick Rock from Compton Lutis Park Piru. One of the staff in charge of my unit, Mr. Burns, A.K.A. Super Dog, was a madman when it came to discipline and punishment and earned his nickname by compelling the hardest of juveniles to conform to the rules. The first day we met, he told me, "You're gonna be here a long time," and soon after he nicknamed me "Sneaky John," because while others fought and argued openly, I preferred the silent attack. For example, when Beto from Pasadena Raymond walked by and said, "Fuck Swan, this Crip," and later that day went to the bathroom, I silently followed and hit him in the face with a rock that I had dressed in a sock, fracturing his nose as I stood over him and said,

"Next time I'ma kill you." Although Super Dog didn't see this and Beto didn't snitch, he knew I did it and sent me to the box for 40 days of torture.

The man who was in charge of the place in solitary confinement demanded that everyone call him "Captain" and made those in the box remain in underclothes while he froze the unit with the cooling system, and following breakfast until 7 p.m., made us "line up." To line up meant to sit on the foot of one's perfectly made-up bed with one hand on each knee all day and if caught "out of position" the caption would take you to one of four special rooms in the back where he'd then force you onto your stomach and hogtie you like a sheep -- an hour for each infraction.

A typical visit to the box was anywhere from one to seven days, but my homie Eggo from Blood Stone Villian and I spent weeks at a time there, and up to six hours tied up. We told the Captain straight up, "Fuck yo rules, we don't give a fuck, and when I see you on the outside, I'm gonna kill you," so he hated us. It wasn't until I saw Twin go home eight months later that I started to think because I had been there three to four months before him, yet he was on his way out, that I needed to bite my tongue and go along to get along which thrilled Super Dog because he badly wanted credit and recognition for taming "Sneaky John." It was like when I saw Twin leave, I also saw something Super Dog desired most, to break me, so I gave him what he wanted to get what I needed.

But after 11 months of role-playing, when my day to go home came, I was summoned to the Director's office, where he told me he wouldn't sign off to release me to my mom because the 77th police chief didn't want me back in Los Angeles. The Director even had a copy of all the letters I had written to Snoopy with particular portions highlighted and said because of those letters he had to concur I had some kind of "hold" over her that needed to break so that she could heal and move on. When he further said he'd discussed it with my mom and she too agreed, I came unglued, yelling, "Fuck all ya'll! I ain't doing shit." When he then said it had been arranged for me to go live with my dad, John-boy, in Rock Island, Illinois, and that he was eager to meet me, I told the Director he could hold me 'til I was 18 or I'd escape, whichever came first, but that I wasn't going to Illinois. So he calmly said he'd give me time to think and decide. It took me three months before I came back to his office and agreed to go, but that was only because my mom promised if I went and completed one semester in school that I could come back home to California. Only she had to say that to convince me to go because the reality was, she had given up custody over me to John-boy as part of the deal.

With the copy of my letters to Snoopy on the Director's desk, I was convinced that she had been setting me up. Plus I was mad at having that sensitive side of me exposed since it didn't fit with the image of being hard, so I never wrote her or answered any of her mail before I left. *Had I had any sense or morals of a man, I would have never thought to take advantage of her or do her harm, and I would have surely protected her from the likes of K. Rock.*

The gang alters one's way of thinking where you believe a homeboy willing to die with or for you is the only friend to trust, and if you love or care for me then you will either help ride for and defend the gang or accept and love my homies the way you love or care for me. The gang also conforms one's belief system to think that others must adapt to gang culture and abandon all others, for how the gang functions and operates is the only way to do so, with no exceptions.

My introduction to such culture at such a young age had me convinced that the structure held by the Swans was not only unique but so fantastic that any outsider should consider themselves blessed to be privy or a part of it. *I would later learn, however, that a gang has no meaning or purpose other than to kill, steal, and destroy, as it kills those thought to be foe, then each other. It steals any chance one has at a fruitful, joyous life and destroys everything and everyone in its wake like a toxic poison.* A poison well hidden behind the power one believes to possess in victory over other gangs, masked behind the glamour we feel as we represent our gang with style and grace. *This is why it took me so long to unmask its truths, and why others so vulnerable and impressionable continue to fall*

prey to gang evolution.

Super Dog volunteered to escort me to the airport in some van with explicit instructions from the Director to watch me get on the plane and wait for it to take off before leaving. While en-route, he offered a lot of good advice on how I could be a success in life if I took the energy invested in the gang and did something positive instead, but I was too nervous about flying on an airplane to pay attention. As it turned out, flying wasn't so bad, just a risk of hijack or engine failure by luck, so by the time I had to catch a second plane, I was eager to get it over with.

When I landed in Iowa State Airport and entered the terminal, I immediately saw a 5'9, slightly bowleg, slim framed with big round eyes, John-boy smiling at me with front teeth missing. The first thing that came to my mind was, "this fool is not my father and I need to shake him quick." As I emerged, he came to rest one arm on my shoulder as if to hug me, but I kept moving to avoid any contact with him, and when

73

he asked me how the flight was, I asked if he wanted me to drive. I pretended that the snowy Illinois streets had no effect on me, a prime example of how gang culture teaches one to act hard to avoid admitting that I was cold as hell. I didn't arrive with anything except the clothes on my back, and when John-boy said he may need to call my mom to help with school clothes, I told him I would take care of it.

A joyous John-boy who believed if it was nice,

you should try it twice.

As we crossed the bridge into Rock Island, he drove to a housing project called the Arsenal Courts, where he rented a three-bedroom apartment furnished with run down, well-worn furniture which looked worse than a spot. It was then that I learned John-boy had a son named Marcus, who was 14 years old my junior, and a daughter named Nicole, who was 13. Both kids were from another lady named Brenda, who lived with him part-time. Brenda lived in her own house just a block up the street from the projects where Marcus and Nicole lived primarily.

The first thing John-boy did was try to control and intimidate me by telling me not to leave my room or the house without his permission, which I found funny because although I had never met him, I had heard plenty of stories from my mom and aunts about how John-boy liked to control and intimidate. So when he commenced his tactics on me, it was already expected, which made me laugh because it was so typical. When he asked me what was so funny, I said I was going to bed and would talk to him in the morning, and when morning came, I woke him up sleeping on his living room sofa, demanding, "Where is the damn phone?" only to learn he didn't have one purposely and relied on the payphone just outside the back door.

As I stood in disbelief, someone knocked on the back door, and that is when I met Marcus and Nicole. I could sense that they dreaded spending time with John-boy, and were always eager to return to their mother's home. They entered like depressed robots, first taking off their snow boots to place behind the door, then jackets to hang on the door, as they beelined straight to the stairs and headed for their individual bedrooms. They were stopped by John-boy who introduced us, otherwise they may have not acknowledged me. My response was, "What's wrong with ya'll?" Then I turned to John-boy and asked, "What did you do to them?" The question provoked a snicker from Nicole as he reacted, offended by the implication. Upstairs, however, they would come out of their shells and give me the rundown.

John-boy was still married to their mom who feared him enough to allow him to collect welfare for the kids. She worked a decent job to take care of them. They could only go to their mom's house on his schedule and approval. Besides having no phone, he also didn't allow television, sugar, junk food, or friendships. They only seemed to know that I was from California and had just gotten out of jail, so I enlightened them with the fact that they were stupid for succumbing to John-boy's dictatorship, and I wouldn't be there long. I asked if their mom would receive money for me and asked for her last name, and then went to the phone booth to place a collect call home to California where my own mom was happy I had made it safe and warned me not to push John-boy too hard. After the call with my mother, I managed to track down Nino and told him of my situation. He got with some homies and sent a Western Union to Brenda for me for $3,500.

83rd and Avalon, the last ones left.

When I called Brenda to inform her, apologizing for not checking with her in advance, she was obviously concerned over John-boy's reaction so I told her to keep him out of my business, as this didn't concern him. I told Brenda that I needed her help to get ready for school, so she agreed to take off work the next day to take me shopping and that is what we did--she even let me drive her car.

Being directed around by Brenda was like being on a date. I treated her like the queen she was, and we had such a wonderful time that we completely lost track of it, but not before she confided in me her regret over getting involved with John-boy because of his controlling and selfish ways. Although they were separated, she still felt trapped by him and helpless to escape and all the while, too scared to even try. I was able to relate because of the tales my own mom had told me about him, and Brenda was relieved to have someone relate as she seemed to draw strength from my own.

When I returned home to John-boy's at about 11 p.m., bags of fresh gear, leftover cash, and happy in good cheer, he demanded who I thought I was "coming down here like you runnin' things," then grabbed me by the throat.

As if I would just let him choke me. I pushed him back off of me, and as he charged, I punched him twice in the face, and he fell to the floor, knocking over chairs to the kitchen table. But he kept coming at me and to avoid hitting him again, I ran around the table yelling, "Ain't nobody scared of you, let's go outside," because I didn't want to tear up the place.

He then told me, "Go to your room," and without thinking, I said, "I ain't doing shit. How dare you put your hands on me!" So he grabbed a broom first, then a mop, breaking each on the wall above my head and around me as if to intimidate me as I stood fists clenched saying over and over again, "Just don't put your hands on me."

Nicole then cried from the stairs, "Daddy, ya'll stop," which seemed to calm him as he gave me this sinister look and told me to "clean up this mess and go to your room."

I picked up my many bags, placed them in the room that I shared with Marcus, then went to the payphone to call my mom and vent about what happened, as I assured her that if he ever put his hands on me again, I would kill him.

Over the next few weeks, John-boy and I rarely spoke to avoid conflict. I had agreed to respect his 10 p.m. curfew rule, so he seemed content for the moment. Since he and Brenda were still legally married, and I had to use her address anyway for school zone reasons, she took off work again to enroll me in Rocky High School, where I insisted that they start me in the 10th grade.

I had already found a weed connection that turned out to be John-boy himself, so I was more relaxed after all the tension. I saw this sister on her porch smoking a joint one evening by herself, walked over, and said, "Let me get in on that."

At first, she frowned at me, then asked if I was John-boy's son. Then she said she just spent her last $10 with John-boy, and since I was the son of "the man" that I could get my own. I took out a wad of cash and told her if she let me smoke, I'd buy the next bag and she agreed, but she didn't want to be seen smoking with me since I was a minor and she could lose her project apartment, so she invited me inside. Her name was Tonya and she was a groundskeeper at the cemetery trying to make it on her own.

So every day thereafter, I'd go to her place to smoke weed, drink beer, and teach her dances that she called "California funk." Tonya opened my eyes to John-boy's hussle, and I came to find out that he supplied the whole projects with weed and had a fleet of women he often entertained. John-boy did his business out of an ice cream truck and sold used cars by day and weed at night.

After learning this, I couldn't resent him so much anymore, so when I'd come in just before 10 p.m., I'd smile and say things like, "slick as snot" and "for the love of money," which melted the tension between us, because he would laugh and assume my sudden fair mood was due to meeting a girl, to which he'd often ask, "Who you sweet on?"

School was going great. I had qualified for a program called "Best," which catered to the top five students in each class, where every day after school we could go to a center set up with computers and take tests for an hour a day, and each test passed would earn us $10. I raked in anywhere from $200 to $300 every week for about two to three months before Best got me and a few other students part-time jobs as groundskeepers in the cemetery where Tonya worked. To me, this was all proof to my mom that I was ready to come home, for in all I had accomplished and achieved I had yet to get the gang out of my heart and soul--not even close.

When the school semester ended with me holding top grades, and it was time to cash in the ticket to come home to California, John-boy told me to, "Go call yo momma," and when I did, she said I was doing so good that she wanted me to complete another semester. So I said okay. Then one night, a few days later in the summer of 1987, I pretended to be going washing, and took all my clothing, paid some lady to drive me across the bridge to Iowa, and jumped on a greyhound headed for California. After a day and a half of traveling, I called my mom, who already knew what was going on, and she just encouraged me to be safe.

This would be yet another significant moment in my life where I was too blinded by the desire to bang to see. I had not only survived well outside the gang but had thrived in a normal, civilized society where I fitted in with regular everyday people doing regular everyday things. I didn't have to hurt anybody, and nobody was out looking to hurt me, so although I was relatively safe, I was restless with the feeling of being alienated from the real world without the gang. I somehow knew that I didn't need the gang, but I felt the gang needed me and was determined not to let them down. Such a determination is what allowed me to conform to basic standards of living while in Rock Island and what drove me to succeed in order to reunite with the gang.

If anyone should wonder how such determination could drive one to become so eagerly desperate to resume a life of chaos and madness, then those who ponder need only be reminded of he who initiated the quest to kill, steal, and destroy.

Six months before my 17th birthday, I made it back to California to see just how much had changed in my absence. For starters, Nate was gone, which pretty much left every man for himself, except Scar, who somehow inherited Nate's sport corvette, 450 SEL Benz, and status in the cocaine game and connections. But instead of a structure of unity and shared wealth, Scar sought a crew of workers who slaved for cash solely for self.

On my first night home, Nino updated me on the basics with explicit instructions not to be a slave for Scar. K. Rock had apparently resumed relations with Scar and earned himself not only a healthy cocaine sack but also a spot on 83rd across from grandma's in a duplex bestowed to James by his own dying mother, which had already proven to remain a constant gold mine for years to come.

My mom had moved from the projects of the Avalon Gardens to a four-bedroom apartment just a block from USC on Jefferson Blvd in another Blood gang neighborhood known as the Fruit Town Brims. So Nino, Mr. Freeze, and I would come to make the trip to 83rd together every morning, then split up to do what it is we each did, sometimes making it back home together or meeting up there in the wee hours of the morning. Nino would add $500 to the cash I brought from Illinois and instruct me to purchase four and a half ounces of cocaine from K. Rock in order to "get rolling," while Freeze would give me a dull chrome 32 revolver pistol and four boxes of bullets, instructing me to "be safe out here." Nino's wife, Tammy, who then lived in Bellflower, was assigned by Nino as my personal driver and who would also make errands on call and keep us abreast of any dangers known.

I was eager to see K. Rock so Tammy drove me on 84th to his house, warning me the whole time, "It ain't the same now that Nate gone. Everyone scandalous now." But I just wouldn't believe, for, in my heart, we were Swan for life. So when my stepmom Gwen let me in to see my boy, I was happy as hell, but when he told me to wait in the living room as he got dressed, then delayed as if he were avoiding me, I became suspiciously concerned because I practically grew up in his room as he did mine, and we shared everything, but now I felt like an outsider.

Then, after much delay, I went and knocked on his room door to ask "what's up?" and informed him that I was trying to get a quarter-pound for $3,500 as homie love. He simply cracked the door, and without showing his face, handed me a flower tray with at least 20 ounces enclosed and yelled "pick five out of that," then reclosed the door, which stung me to a state of frozen silence.

Subsequent my pause, I went back into the living room to examine the works, noting each was holey and off white, which I knew meant that the cocaine had too much cut and would crumble as I broke to sell, so I went back and knocked on K-rocks door to advise him that I was "cool" and didn't want it. He told me to leave the flower tray on the floor and wait so we could ride in his El Camino Thunder to Fremont High to talk to some girls, but I told him I'd catch him later, feelings hurt as I was forced to realize that Tammy was right all along. She must have known because as soon as I got into her four-door dark blue Pinto, she said, "I told you, but don't trip, you don't need them. They all want your heart, so fuck them." This almost made me break down and cry because I felt like something was lost, and I was looking for something I couldn't find. *In that moment, all I wanted was to tell Snoopy that I was sorry.*

As we departed, Tammy asked me to roll with her to Bellflower for a moment and the next thing I knew, she was pulling over on Florence Ave in front of a supermarket, swearing to me that one of the cars that pulled into its parking lot belonged to an East Coast Crip she knew personally. Encouraging me to "get his ass," I snapped out of the emotional fog, looked around, and told her to meet me on the next block up the avenue. I got out of the vehicle, entered the parking lot full of cars, went up to the blue Cadillac coupe in the handicap zone, and opened fire with the 32 four times point blank at its driver. My training caused me to save two rounds to aid my escape in the event of difficulty, and as I fled up the alley, I suddenly felt alive, like I had reclaimed that dark power one feels when taking something from someone else.

As soon as I sat back in that pinto seat, I laughed at the wimp, who not ten minutes earlier, had sunk into sorrow over lost friendship. *Unknown to me at the time, it was natural to feel sorrow or grief for loss of anything significant or important to me, as these are the most essential emotions, which make us human. Gang culture strips away all sense of humanity by reprogramming us to regard feelings of sadness, sorrow, emotional hurt and pain, as being soft or weak. This type of manipulative conditioning instills psychological confusion where feelings of anguish and woe are replaced by the mask of anger, revenge, and covet to inflict pain on others.*

With this successful mission, my senses refocused to adapt back into the gang culture, and suddenly, selling crack became a second priority, so I used the bulk of the cash I had to stock ammunition and update my wardrobe. When my mom told me that when grandma died, Freeze and Nino lived in the apartment for months thereafter rent-free as if they owned the unit, daring the landlord to remove them. The sheriffs forced them out, provoking them to kick the walls out inside the apartment in protest before finally leaving. I began to sense their silent rage at being forced from 83rd during our morning rides from the Fruit Town Brims to the east side. I gathered in the sense that, the daily travels made them feel more like visiting outsiders rather than natives, but, *I somehow came to enjoy the relief of not having innocent family or loved ones at risk of bullets meant for one of us,* and relished in the escape to the west side after a wild day of terrorizing on the east.

I acquired a 38 snub nose and used the back area of my old apartment, the area between Snoopy's old bedroom window and grandma's kitchen window, to create a stash for weapons and other contraband, as well as a post position where I'd sit on milk crates to patrol Avalon or kill time. Just less than a half a block down and across the street, K. Rock had made his spot jumpin' with Hot Dog, Noon, Popeye, Moe, Bill, K-Swiss, and James' little brother, Garthen, all working for him to sell his crack. These were all homies who were a grade behind us when in Mrs. Belcher's class, so although we grew up together, none of these kids were yet factors in the gang and were starting out as young dealers working for K. Rock. Despite the height of the gang war at this time, Swan territory had managed to spread where the borderlines were recognized as from Florence Avenue to Manchester Avenue, and from Main Street to Central Avenue, which roughly is a fair size sandbox square requiring 24 hour protection and guard.

Being shot at or getting shot was common, and with the murder rate still on the rise, snitching had become a bigger threat than getting killed. With so many upcoming homies looking for status and recognition who had yet to be tested, it became a protective factor not to go on missions or put in work with homies you had never worked with before. So initially, whenever I went to or around K. Rock's spot, I avoided discussing or speaking on events that concerned any type of shootings and learned to listen from background positions to assess who talked too much or not enough.

Within 60 days of being back, K-rock would get pulled over in thunder by sheriffs and punch one of the deputies in the face earning himself an assault charge. Suddenly, I saw an opportunity to take over his spot because, in his absence, none of the workers in his crew were able to put or keep cocaine in the spot, as many customers loyal or accustomed to buying crack at James's house sought other connections to score. So within a week of K. Rock's arrest, I took $1,000 to K. Wack, who served me with powder cocaine, hired my OG homegirl to help me cook it into crack, then went to James's house to implement my own structure, and announce that I was taking over.

Because I had previously shot James in one of Nate's spots years earlier, it wasn't hard to take control, and he didn't object because he knew I'd shoot him again. But mainly, James loved to lock himself in his room with some female companion, get naked, and smoke crack. The deal was he would get a gram of crack a day and a line of credit. The primary perk of having me as a dealer meant that when customers came to buy, he could offer them the comfort and the safety of his home in order to help smoke their crack as host. I didn't give K. Rock's abandoned crew drugs to sell for me--instead, I sold them their own for whatever they had to spend, ensuring to double their money each time. I didn't particularly hang in the spot like most, as I was out on duty doing what I believed was keeping the hood safe, but I made sure the spot was always open for business, even leaving up to $200 of crack for James to sell in my absence. There were times when he'd vanish for days due to oversmoking, but he already knew what consequence awaited him if he was caught, so despite his Houdini act, he always returned with my money in full.

With the gang culture's insatiable demand for shootings and murders on both sides, many Swans were in fear of being charged with homicide by being snitched on and began selling cocaine more than they dared gang banging. They'd rely on work they put in years before to maintain status and respect, but this would only lead to them being robbed by other Swans like me who resented homies who'd limit the use of guns to protect themselves or their spots from being robbed yet wouldn't use those same guns to keep Crips at bay or avenge a homie's death.

Then came a mixture of hustlers who always seemed to be around when drugs were needed for buying and selling, but vanished when it was time to shoot or dodge bullets. In the gang, a basic charge of or failure to respond would undoubtedly ruin one's entire career, for when Crips were suspected or identified one had to react with some form of violence to represent, preferably murder to uphold the gang's infamous terror.

So it was no surprise that after about two months of operating from James' house, making fine money, a crowd had gathered on and around 83rd and Avalon to watch as an ambulance scraped a motorcycle rider off the pavement after colliding with a passing car while fleeing from police. It'd parked just before the entrance into the Orbit Motel, where four Crips in a Suzuki, clad in blue, were flashing Crip hand signs to some of the crowd members. As I crept undetected through the back of the apartments next to the motel and Avalon, I confronted the Jeep members with both my 32 and my 38 snub nose, sending one back passenger over the side into the street, the other into the driver's lap as the passenger immediately returned fire, all with the police less than 10 feet away. I was so swift, the police initially believed the Jeep members were shooting into the crowd, which assisted in my escape, except that these dudes were real hardcore Crips. They drove down and around the alley hunting me as the police hunted them, sending me in hiding scared to death for not being able to make it to my stash to reload.

That day, I thanked the police in prayer as that Suzuki eventually sped off to avoid capture because those dudes weren't scared at all, and their wounded made them mad enough to risk finding me. I learned two things this day: one was that my fear of shooting a 38 was highly overrated; the other was instead of carrying wads of cash, I needed to start carrying bullets for reloading, because I never wanted to feel that scared and helpless again.

Freeze would later allow me to bask in that smile of approval I had come to relish, and with only him could I share the feeling of doubt and fear as I ran from pursuit. He would reassure me that I'd "be alright" and warned me to be extra careful because now that "they" saw me, "they" would be back. Before 1987 would end, both Nino and Freeze would catch cases and end up in prison for the first time, and for the first time, I was truly on my own, left with the warning of Freeze's "they'll be back," to give me the inner fear to survive.

With the commencement of 1988, I was widely recognized as a young original gangster, an OG, who filled the shoes of Mr. Freeze in his absence. I was now responsible for protecting not only the neighborhood but also the younger homies who regarded me as some role model to live up to. I didn't know it at the time but the older OGs like Tweet, Rub, Dog, Bird, Reno, Monk, S.G, Tommy, Joe, and a vast amount of others, well knew who I was and had already embraced me into the gang long before I had ever met them. When these dudes were released from prison, they came straight to 83rd looking for me for safe survival, and I was always excited to be in the presence of these legendary Swans who all assured me that in prison, I was loved, respected, and known as a "killer."

To a 17-year-old teenager, such compliments were today's equivalent of Kim Kardashian unexpectedly showing up at some unknown person's house, work, or school and giving them instant fame and attention for years to come. *The recognition of these dudes served as a negative influence, which promoted and encouraged my psychopathic behaviors. Had I received the same praise, attention, and acknowledgment for obtaining or holding a job or even finishing school, then I would have done that for the mere affection instead of terrorizing victims.*

Hot Dog would prove to have the most promise out of the younger homies I entertained because he was vigilant, listened well, and adhered to instructions without question, so I regarded him as equal and spent extra care grooming him into the gang. Because he had had open-heart surgery as a kid, I was always extra protective of him--plus his mom, Bobby, would always ask me to "take care of my baby," as we left for a day of adventure, which I did.

Since being shot in '85, I had ceased to wear much red, and by '88 I had stopped altogether, so Hot Dog had followed suit. Gang culture had evolved anyhow--colors didn't matter much anyway because professional gang members learned, knew, and remembered faces, so those clad in red or blue were either diehard or wanna-be members starving to be recognized or accepted. Either way, the face told the truth, and my job was simply to read each to determine. I guess cowboys from the old Western days could best relate and knew as much, because a weather-worn face of a man with serious eyes that didn't miss much coupled with either a scar or wrinkles told you that this person was dangerous and no fool, while the baby clean face of a smiling guy told you he didn't have much life experience. Not only did I teach Hot Dog this belief, but I proved its truth by having him post on one corner safe behind some parked car, while he hit up or banged on suspected gang members passing down Avalon with his innocent light face, while I posted on the next block where they'd have to pass, and if he waived his hands in the air it meant that the passers were out of bounds, and I'd emerge to unload 12 or more rounds from two pistols, reload, and repeat the plot.

However, when I'd switched positions with Hot Dog, people weren't as quick or open to admit to being a Crip when I hit them up or banged on them. I also taught Hot Dog how to enter Crip territory and shoot a target successfully the same way Freeze had taught me how to convincingly lie to police using bogus names to avoid being recorded on their gang file and how to resist being detained altogether by using shortcuts or alley mazes to lose police in time to stash weapons.

One afternoon while coming home from the Market Street swap meet in Inglewood, Hot Dog would side-swipe another car trying to switch lanes. We were on Manchester Ave short of crossing Hoover Street and forced to pull into the corner market to assess damages as well as exchange information. A crowd gathered, including the police. Because the crowd was majority Crip, they somehow easily knew we were out of bounds, thus, eased closer to where we were parked stranded. Hot Dog had long since discovered that the impact of the crash killed the battery and engine in his four-door glasshouse. He was obviously nervous as he exchanged information and in near panic as the police quickly geared up to leave after seeing that everyone was okay.

As soon as the last of the two police cars departed, members of the crowd decided to move in to pounce. But minutes before, I had commanded Hot Dog to "pop the hood" in time to see that one of the battery cables had broken off the head, so I touched the cable to its broken part, then said "try it," and as it immediately started, Hot Dog's face, heart, and spirit lit up with joy and happiness from knowing rescue, and as soon as I jumped in, we sped off.

I sat in the back seat smiling through the center of the back window at angry Crips. The fortune we both praised within sealed our bond as friends in addition to homies, and when he asked how "I knew" exactly what to do at exactly the right time, I told him the importance of being calm to be able to think in times or moments of crisis, and how one of my most loved and respected OG homies Hulk form Nine Doose Bishop always taught me that in every situation, the person(s) most confused has less control, and shared the true significance for belief in such a principle.

Another time thereafter, while posted on Avalon where the old dairy market was, in the driveway of the apartments that sit well off the boulevard, Hot Dog, the G-homie Bip P, and I were posted on crates about to smoke weed when a Hispanic F-13 came walking by. He and Hot Dog started arguing, as Hot Dog was mad that he was "walking over here" knowing the brawl that Woofey and I had kicked off with them over one of the arcade games in that dairy weeks prior, which caused an ongoing dispute between members where homies on both sides were taking fades on site. They were about equal size and age, and when Hot Dog punched him, he looked stunned and confused at first, but then took brass knuckles out from one of his Dickie pockets, put them on, and began swinging to bash Hot Dog's skull in, sending him in retreat as his attacker advancement, causing him to fall on his buttocks.

As Hot Dog tried to stand, the F-13 soldier came close to straddling him as he focused, in position, to make one of the nine punches he already threw and missed land. But by then, I had already a metal crate in motion, slapping him square on the side of his face and head, putting him out cold for moments. He woke up dazed and baffled. As Hot Dog jumped up, he stood over Big P demanding, "Where you from?" since the G-homie didn't help him, but the G-homie Big P started laughing as he licked the blunt and said, "You shouldn't of fired on that man if you couldn't knock him," continuing to laugh as Hot Dog stormed off mad, wanting and expecting me to follow, yet even more upset when I didn't.

After allowing the rival member to leave with his life and the smoke session with the G-homie Big P, I caught up with Hot Dog. He had calmed down, laughed, and then thanked me for helping him. I used the experience to stress the requirement that he had to "hold his own" in the gang, otherwise, he'd get ran over and threw, elaborating in-depth on how the fight he just experienced could, should, or would of went had he initiated a true hold your own attitude prior to the moment he struck. Hot Dog would prove to have digested and applied this concept extremely well as he groomed through the culture of gang life.

Hot Dog, Noon, Bill, Moe, Popeye, and Lil Lump would all be compelled, as part of some neighborhood intervention by parents trying to save these kids from following me through gang life, to enroll and attend Drew Junior High School, which was well governed by an array of Crips. I had long since had my dispute at Drew when a year or two prior to 1988, Freeze's mom, my aunt Suga, took me to enroll in Drew as part of a court mandate. But while in the enrollment office, I had to make Suga pretend she wasn't with me and leave me there, so she could make it safely to the car, then I had to shoot my way out with that nine-shot 22 Freeze had given me. Because of that, I already knew that all the little

104

homies would have problems at that school and suggested to them they either pack a gun or don't go.

So for the next week, they all came running home to me in the spot by lunch because Crips pressed them, then made them "hit the gate," and they had to get out of Drew to avoid a stomp down. The next week when they tried my advice of sticking together at lunch to fight back, some older Crips outside of Drew enrollment began coming to the school, and whoever they were terrified them more than usual so they begged me for days to meet them out front of the school.

So, one day I did meet them outside of the school. While sitting in my nova with my 32 and 38 pistols, I began to call brothers. I got there almost an hour early so that I could park right in front with sure getaway access, but when school came out for the day nothing special went on--at first. After the homies had been out front with me for about 10-15 minutes flirting with girls, a pack of 7-10 Crips in blue came out of nowhere with angry faces charging directly at us, or more so at me. I told everybody to get in the car and just when members of the crowd got within three feet of me, I whipped the 32 from my back pocket and took calm and confident aim at the faces, one shot to every face in sequence, and by the 4th shot, had whipped the 38 out smoothly.

But by then the gang and school crowd had scattered like scared pigeons in a park that were confronted by excited dogs out to play. As I made my way to the driver's seat of the nova, I quickly reloaded the spent bullets putting empty shells in my pocket while putting the gear in drive, and eased off in departure when the school security pulled alongside me with only a driver, demanding that I "cut off the engine and get out of the vehicle."

Without thought, I shot three rounds from the 38 into the passenger window at the driver then gunned the 350 engine up Manchester Ave, over 100 miles an hour, before I reached Central Ave. A second security car followed and tracked my route. When I made the right on Central Ave, followed by a slick left turn off onto 85th, and made it to Wadsworth Ave, the security car was about half a block behind me. We could hear real police sirens in the distance, so I told everybody to get ready to bail out once I made it to the back of the spot on 83rd. I knew I was risking exposure by leading the chase to the area of the spot, but I also knew this was a serious situation, and the only sure way of ensuring everyone's safe escape was by this route that I had come to know and rely on so well.

As I brought the spinning of the rear tires and reeving of the engine with its 400 turbo transmission to the alley behind the spot, I had almost a block distance from the security car so I told everyone to split up into different spots and to not come out until night. As they bailed to flee to the right, I ran left, to the side of the spot onto the brick wall that divided James's house from the duplexes, then climbed up the window onto the roof where I lay hidden in the tree's thick branches that covered one section of the front house. This is where I kept my rifles and backup ammunition and where I hid almost every time I did something I was scared of or was wanted for. It was where I had always survived.

Since no one knew its place, I knew I was safe. I lay hidden in the tree behind the many leaves as the police searched for anyone they could find, and when the sunset, I came back down to discover that the police had broken the window of the nova to enter and someone had ripped out the entire fuse box under the steering wheel so that the car wouldn't start. But after replacing the fuse box, the car was good as new.

By the end of the next day, I got chased again while driving the nova, by police who knew it, and soon I, if caught, was on the hot sheet. So, after I evaded the police, I went and sold the rust gold nova to Solo for $600, of which he only gave me $200, and because he was Poobear's little brother, I told him that the police were looking for the driver of the Nova and why. But Solo was a well-groomed young Swan so he didn't care. However, two weeks later, he would argue that he shouldn't have to be responsible to pay the balance after being detained for three days and questioned about the driver who sold him the car, as he was wanted for attempted murder. Plus, he lost the nova to impound so I let him off the hook as a reward for not snitching me out and for being a young G.

With the shooting at Drew Jr. High School, Hot Dog, Noon, Bill, Moe, Popeye, and Lil Lump knew they couldn't return, and when their parents learned why, of course, they blamed me and forbade any of their kids from "hanging around that boy."

Bernice, Noon's mom, would see me on 83rd and either summon me or come up to me, place her hand on my forehead, and pray, warning me that if I continued to live by the gun, I'd die by the gun. She'd often mention my grandma too, and as she did her prayer, I would keep a watchful eye on the boulevard to prevent from being shot down while slippin'.

Then one afternoon, not ten minutes after Bernice had prayed for me, leaving a symbol of the cross on my forehead with olive oil, Tammy and I were out front of James's spot smoking weed when the red traffic light caught several cars in halt. Tammy calmly said, as she took the joint I passed to her, "Them crabs in that black car, I know them." And before I could exhale the smoke I inhaled, I ran hunched over to the vehicle caught in the traffic jam and saw the female driver in her blue and white sweatsuit looking in fear at my sudden presence. The passenger was still oblivious, hiding his blue sports hat in his lap as I politely walked to his side of the car to punish him with all six rounds from my 38. When I made it back to hit the joint, the woman was still screaming before taking off or realizing that she had been spared.

Early the next morning when I made it to the spot, Noon, Bill, Popeye, Moe, Lil Lump, Garthen, and a reluctant Hot Dog were all in the back where Noon had a prayer circle going on, and when they saw me Noon said, "We decided we don't want to hang around you because you shoot too many people so somebody is gonna kill you." I told them that was "cool" but this is a spot so they needed to find somewhere else to hang out. Noon said they didn't mind selling crack but "shooting people every day" was too much. As I opened the spot, I began to feel eerie over what Noon had said because I knew it all came from his mom, Bernice, who was a spiritual lady, and the more I pondered on it the more I felt afraid, so I went to the roof where I hid out convincing myself that I was evading the death predicted. Then in the far distance, I heard gunshots, and as they grew louder, I peeked through the thick tree leaves to see Noon, Hot Dog, and Popeye run off Avalon down 83rd as a tan Chevy mini blazer followed. A passenger sat on the door of the window sill and was taking pop shots as the driver guided the chase.

While laughing to myself at the look of terror on Noon's face as he ran in his tight-fitting Dickies, I took one of the rifles and shot 21 times off of the roof to pepper the passenger's back and side with a string of 22 hollow point bullets that ended the chase. I would later insist they continue to uphold the decision to not "hang" around me because they weren't cut out for this life; however, I made an exception for Hot Dog because he appeared not to be sold by Noon's decision--plus he had already grown on me as a friend.

Seeing me embrace Hot Dog made Noon, Bill, Popeye, and Lil Lump try hard to gain my approval and acceptance.

They would come together to buy a 38 pistol, but before they could even shoot it, Popeye was caught by police with it and ended up in LP followed by camp. Then one night while at the Vermont drive-in, in a rented van that Beagle and Lil Dan got from a crackhead who let us use it in exchange for drugs, we went into the snack bar after smoking too much weed, and when we emerged, we were confronted by 15-20 Crips who told us we couldn't be there.

Before anyone could react or say anything, Noon stepped forward to announce, "I'm Big Nooney lok from 84 Swan, I'll knock out yo biggest homeboy right now!" His statement intimidated them enough to allow us to leave without incident. This showed me that Noon was at least down for the gang, so I embraced him for his willingness to represent by allowing him to hold my 32 after I closed the spot and went home to shower and change clothes.

But one day I returned to discover that my 32 was gone. Apparently, Noon had let Bill hold it, and when the police came, he panicked and ran, throwing the gun onto the roof of an apartment where it went off, leading the police to think that he was crazy enough to shoot at them. When he was apprehended, the fire department was called to retrieve the gun from the rooftop, and Bill was arrested. When the police later did a ballistic check, Bill was threatened with accessory and conspiracy charges if he didn't tell them who the owner of the gun was, but he didn't snitch me out, and his tale of "I bought it from a smoker" eventually won them over, so he too ended up in camp.

The story of Bill's arrest had everyone laugh so I didn't mind losing my gun, plus I had learned to love the feel of the 38, which is why I lent the 32 instead. Within a week of its loss, as we were out front of James's spot one afternoon, my older homie Earl pulled up on 83rd, turned down his music, and said, "Its some crabs in the house right next to the alley on 84th behind the wash house."

Hot Dog demanded, "Why you come to tell us?"

Earl said, "I came to tell Bleep," staring right at me.

I got into Earl's car telling Hot Dog to "stay here, I'll be back."

I had Earl drop me off on Towne Ave and 84th down the street from the target, and before I closed the car door he said, "These not no young dudes so be careful." I told him I got this and marched the block to the house in question which was fenced off and covered by plants that entwined the entire gate. The only view of the house itself or its yard was by and through the entrance gate that was clear.

As I reached that gate, I saw a man in blue on the front porch on the phone. The "clink" of me opening that gate to enter caused him to look up, drop the phone, and reach for his back pocket, but I opened fire with all rounds sending him slamming backward into the bar front door then down where he was hidden by the brick porch wall.

As I released the revolver to put the empty shells in my pocket and reload, the bar door flew open and another dude with what looked and sounded like a 45 started shooting at me, sending me running from the threshold of the yard gate to the alley as bullets cut through the plants on the gate. I was determined to finish my reload and buss again as I squat at the alley entrance, but I saw my big homie, Monkey Man, emerge from behind a parked car with the legendary chrome Thompson machine gun Swans were said to have, and that I had heard about since I was a kid. He opened fire, but it jammed after three shots. By then I was reloaded and came in time to shoot the guy who was about to exit the yard and shoot Monkey Man as he struggled to unjam the Thompson. Monkey Man then told me to "leave" as he entered the yard and unloaded the 60 round drum, playing the trigger like an instrument, and as I made it back to 83rd, I could still hear him getting off shots as everyone asked me, "What is that?" and "What happened?" knowing, however, that my lips were sealed.

Later that night, Tweet came on 83rd, gave me a 357 magnum, and said, "Hold this but don't get caught with it." Of course I was scared since I had only just gotten accustomed to my 38, but I never let on such fear to anyone. To further mask the fear, I gave Hot Dog the 38 to hold. I guessed that he was as scared as I was for the same reason, but we would both be forced to face our fears as three carloads of Crips came up 83rd yelling, "Fuck Swan," shooting at anyone that moved.

As Tweet and the other homies took cover, I stepped into the street to confront the passing visitors, greeting the first car with two shots of thunder. The noise, flame, and kick excited the hell out of me, and although I missed my target, I quickly learned that I had to aim lower because the recoil made the gun jump. So with the next four shots, I caused one of the three vehicles to sideswipe a parked car in an effort to escape, and with Hot Dog backing me up shooting the 38, we turned their hit into an escape for their lives, which gained even more praise and recognition from the gang since Tweet saw us in action. I used the event to show Hot Dog how he could have been more effective by not shooting from standing on the curb and how to be more accurate with every shot.

The next day, I had Ethel go to Big 5 to get two boxes of 357 hollow points and learned that the police response to me unloading that magnum was a lot quicker than with the 22, 25, 32, or even the 38, because the impact was more gruesome. This was a fear I should have held onto for dear life, because the power I felt surpassed any I'd ever felt before and turned me into something or someone that only the devil himself could have created--something that only evil could love, accept, or even understand, which is why only my gang could stomach my vile behaviors.

Some days later, after pulling an all-nighter in the spot, Lil Dan came in the early morning in his green cutlass Oldsmobile with Hot Dog and Gadget looking for me to buy a $50 sack of chronic to smoke with them before they went to Fremont High School. They knew that because I was flushed with cash I would. Before getting into the back seat, Lil Dan asked me not to ride in his car with my gun since the car was registered in his mother's name, so out of respect I left the 357 and the 38 at James' spot and jumped in the back seat with Hot Dog as I began to count and organize cash from last night's score.

After leaving the weed house on 80th and Main, we were coming up 79th between San Pedro and Towne Avenue when Gadget suddenly said, "Back up real quick, we just passed a crab," and as Lil Dan did, Gadget got out to confront some guy walking towards San Pedro, and Hot Dog got out to join him. After at least five minutes from the moment we stopped, I finished counting money to look up and see that they were still conversing with the suspected Crip as Lil Dan was busy rolling up the weed, so I told him to "let me out," and as I emerged, the suspected Crip looked at me and then took off running as both Hot Dog and Gadget gave immediate chase.

But I was swift to catch and pass them, and as I caught up with the runner inches from grabbing him at the collar of his shirt, he suddenly had a pistol in hand, and as I slowed down while turning around to retreat, he shot me through the right wrist into the right leg, then chased us all back towards the car. I jumped a fence into a yard to hide behind a vehicle in the driveway as the shooter then turned and ran back the other way out of sight. Furious, I insisted Lil Dan take me home since my mom was a nurse and I had no intentions of reporting the gunshot. As we smoked the weed, I regretted leaving my guns at the spot and vowed to never be so stupid as to confront someone without one ever again.

As we made it to USC on Jefferson Blvd, we got pulled over by the police, and when they discovered that I was shot, they had a theory that someone in the car shot me by accident and tried to sway me to concur; however, I had already told Lil Dan to say he found me shot on their way to school, and I begged for a ride home. Then with over $2,000 stuffed in my Levi jeans, the police then swore I was shot robbing someone. I pretended the pain was worse than it was, gave a fake name and address, then left in an ambulance. By the time they made it to the City of Angels, I had already had my mom pick me up as I waited out front.

You would think getting shot a second time, and not by just a single shot from a mere 22 pistol, but by a Crip who wasn't yet a vicious and cold-blooded killer, would have turned me grateful or at least led me to appreciate life's blessings.

Sadly, however, this experience traumatized me to the point where the thought of being so vulnerable sent me to panic, and the only thing that could or would calm me is a gun, which included at least two rounds of reload.

Without a pistol, I couldn't feel safe or in control, and I lost confidence in the belief that a homie could or would protect me, as this was a duty only I could ensure for myself. You would think this experience would tenderize that hard image I built in some sort of compassion and understanding, but all it did was hold me shellshocked in anger, resentment, and fear, facing PTSD symptoms without treatment.

This was yet another significant moment in my life because, in this experience, I became psychotic, delusional by the self-created belief that "when you stop shootin' you get shot." So I was determined to keep shooting until all the Crips were dead or until the screws came out of the gun. *I had no idea that I was self-destructing, poisoning the minds and lives of everyone who admired me and those I opposed, while simultaneously torturing the loved ones of those victimized by*

compelling them to endure what mess I had left, diminishing
any real skill or gift I had by becoming more and more a part
of the gang culture.

I had my mother take and drop me back off on 83rd with the 22 slug still in my leg as it was too deep for the doctors to extract. I learned immediately that I couldn't hold or shoot the magnum or the 38 since my best shot came from my injured right hand, so I told James to spread word to all the smokers that I had cash and a healthy issue of crack for a small pistol, almost four times worth the rate, and within an hour, Ethel came with a black 22 magnum nine-shot pistol still in the box, and a box of 22 hollow point long bullets, which got her a bonus.

Ethel was a senior citizen addicted to crack who always packed a 357 magnum and was infamous for bussin' on anyone who dared cross or try to mistreat her. She lived on 82nd off Avalon and watched me grow up. When I was about 13, Ethel taught me about the seriousness of business. One day in 1984, she came to score crack on 83rd, and after giving me her money, I told her some slick unrelated tale, gave her the purchase, and then insisted she never paid for it. After 10 minutes of her being confused while checking and rechecking her bra, purse, and panties, I said, "You paid me already, I'm just playing with you."

She responded by immediately pulling her magnum out of that oversized purse she fancied, cocked the hammer, and wickedly responded, "Don't play with me. If you want something to play with then shit in yo hand and play with that cause I will thrill yo ass."

So I learned not to ever play with business or Ethel, and I learned to adopt her principal down to the very language in admonishment. The only thing is, when you commence such practice and belief at such a young age, you learn to take everything and everyone seriously all the time, and by the age of 17, you done flunked P.E. because you don't play.

I immediately fell in love with my new 22 and wrapped an ace bandage on my injured wrist to reclaim that precise shot I had become infamous for. To add security to that feeling of not packing a 357 magnum or 38 special, I carried a paper bag half full of extra bullets, so when me, Noon, and Hot Dog walked to Jimbos on 81 and Avalon for tacos and burgers, I felt pretty safe. The OG homie, Swanny Bird, had just got out of Y.T.S. (Youth Training School) for Wheaty From East Coast's murder, and when he met up with us at Jimbo's, we all hit it off, but more so Bird and I since we both loved guns and got a thrill out of face shots. Plus, I was excited Bird already knew who we were and was looking for us.

Within the hour, there were about 20 homies out front waiting on their food as the sun was just about to set. Suddenly, a car in traffic coming up Avalon Blvd in the lane closest to the curb toward 82nd came yelling to greet, "Big Noon, what's up Blood?"

But in my delusional thoughts it sounded like, "What that Hoover Crip like cuzz," so I came out the waist as homies had already begun to take cover from the passing vehicle which was going about 40 miles an hour and I shot all nine shots with excellent aim and rhythm, hitting the passenger seven times in a perfect line from his shoulder to his waist as the car sped off. I remember as I was shooting Bird was watching me smiling, and when I finished he said, "You a better shot than me," which boosted my ego.

As I immediately reloaded and grabbed my food from the Chinese lady who ranted, "you no come here no more," over and over, we hit the alley going to 83rd when someone coming from there yelled, "Blood why ya'll shoot me" and come to find, it was one of my childhood friends, Ellroy, who was bleeding bad. He knew us all well and demanded to know who shot him. The G-homie, Big P, intervened to convince Ellroy to focus on his injury and going to a hospital, so he decided to insist he be allowed to hit Big P's 40 ounce before, and while doing so, passed out, hitting the ground as the bottle burst sending beer one way and a pool of his bright red blood that had built up in his long sleeve white t-shirt spilling over like a lake the other way.

The whole time Bird was still smiling, which wasn't surprising since he was one of the homies responsible for training Freeze and had absolutely no regard for life, not even his own. Bird then said, "Let's get out the hood because he'll be stinking by morning." But Big P went to get someone to call an ambulance for the boy, which ultimately saved his life. As for me, I regretted seeing Ellroy shot up, but I dealt with it by convincing myself that he deserved it for hanging out the window of a moving car drunk, yelling like a fool, knowing full well that we were at the height of a gang war and many homies had already died just like that.

I gave Bird the 357 magnum with the same admonishment that the OG homie Tweet gave to me, telling Bird, "Don't get caught with it." With Hot Dog carrying the 38, he, Noon, Bird, and I became inseparable. Yet despite this, Hot Dog and Noon both lived with a single mom and were bound by curfew. So by 11 p.m., they were in the house at home while Bird and I hung out in the streets at night, completely obsessed by gang banging, and we quickly established a bond that mirrored the bond Freeze and I had.

Up until this point, I had always spared females who were Crips or down for the gang in blue, because when it came to gang violence I had always believed it was a man's or boy's dispute. However, Bird told me about killing Wheaty and doing time for it because not only was Wheaty a female OG Criplett, but she was one who apparently killed, shot, and set up to be either shot or killed many Swans and other Bloods. To Bird, killing her was personal because she got more Bloods killed then many of the guys in her own gang. This rationale altered my belief and added to what I already was, something God himself would have struck down from existence had it not been for his vow of mercy and forgiveness. Bird made the murder of women caught in the gang culture appear necessary and appealing.

As 1988 persisted, one sunny afternoon while hanging on 83rd, we got word that Hoover Crips, now criminals, were having a funeral at the church on 83rd and San Pedro for one of their OG homies who was said to have died from being poisoned by his wife. Bird told the messenger to convey that they could conduct the service then leave out of respect for the dead, and we all agreed.

However, as the Hoovers gathered in various cars, at least 100 members stood in the middle of 83rd street yelling, "hoo, hoo, hoo" in union repeatedly, and it rang like a bullhorn. Bird, Hot Dog, and I immediately began walking towards the disruptive crowd, and by the time we crossed Towne Ave, Tweet and several other homies were also headed into the crowd.

But several police cars came out of nowhere and everyone with guns ran to stash them somewhere nearby, and when we returned, the police had half of 83rd, between Towne and San Pedro Ave, blocked off while other officers conducted pat-down searches on all of us, while preventing us from crossing the yellow tape used to limit crossing to confront the excited Hoovers who got even louder with the "hoo, hoo, hoo" chant.

Suddenly, Noon, in only a pair of old brown Dickies that were cut into shorts and were too tight-fitting, and a pair of old Fila sneakers handed down by Scar, came walking by dripping wet from the shower, passed the police, and went under the yellow tape without interruption.

As Noon reached the parking area of the church where K. Wack's bright red 64 Chevy was parked, dozens of Hoovers came at him. Noon threw punch after punch, and all Hoovers who had come in contact with his fists fell until there was a pile of at least 15 bodies at his feet. Then Dookie came through the alley into the yard to get off one shot from a 25 pistol which hit some unlucky Hoover in the face, and the police ran to protect Noon thinking it was the Hoovers who had shot at him.

That's when all hell broke loose as Swans from all over went and positioned themselves at every possible exit to inflict whatever damage they could as Hoovers left the church in escape. I split up from Bird and Hot Dog in the chaos and found myself with Money B on 79th and San Pedro, hoping that one of the fleeing cars would take this back route. Moments later, Ernest from 62 East Coast Crip came along in his Cadillac. I took the 45 colt from Money B and just as he cruised by, opened fire through his passenger window while walking alongside his car, continuing to shoot as he drifted into ongoing traffic, crashing into another vehicle followed by a constant blow of his car horn as he lay dead held up on and by the steering wheel.

The OG big homie, Shadey Gradey, certified Noon this day, crowning him with deserving respect as Big Noon, but for this title, he would rise to the top of the Hoovers hit list. For the very next day, and some thereafter, Hoovers would be lying in wait for him to come home and leave messages for the little kids out front to convey to Noon. That told us that somebody we knew, who lived in the hood, was selling us out to be killed and my best guess was that it had to be a female, which made Bird's rationale hold more truth in my eyes.

Later at a meeting held in the back of James's spot, the OG big homie Pollar Bear, warned us about the Hoovers and how in all his years of banging the Hoovers were the most vicious of Crips that he ever had to go against, so we "better get ready." As soon as he said that, we heard shots up the street, which turned out to be Poo Bear being slain by a lone Hoover who, in his disguise as an addict, walked on 83rd into the heart of the hood and murdered my homie in execution.

Poo Bear's murder sent the Swan gang killing rate to a level beyond the ordinary gang killings because he was so well-loved. His murder also caused dispute and resentment among Swans because some believed that other homies "let" Poo Bear die as he did by not protecting him while on 83rd. Some harbored such feelings because those who were there further allowed the gunman to slaughter Poo Bear then just walk away.

All of the resentment and hate from the pain and blame caused Tweet and the OG big homie Dog to single out homies who didn't or rarely put in work in a theme called "buster week," which entailed that they either go kill--not merely shoot--a Crip or get beat and ran out the hood. Poo Bear's murder had any and everybody who lived in the hood going to kill Crips from all over, and those forced to do so were too scared of Dog and Tweet to refuse or say no.

I was personally offended by Poo Bear's murder simply because someone had come on 83rd and I wasn't able to confront them. But with all the shootings and murders going on, I had my chance daily since every day some Crip gang came to retaliate. With every attempt, Bird, Hot Dog, and I upheld the gang's reputation for turning an attempted hit by Crip gangs on one of the homies into some desperate escape to save their own lives. Bird and I were marksmen with pistols, and we delighted in rapid-fire and swift reload. Bird would eventually be seen by police shooting a Crip in cold blood as he used a payphone on Manchester and San Pedro Ave, blowing the life out of him with that 357 magnum, then leading police on a chase with Dog before being caught and arrested, but without the pistol.

Two months later, police saw me on 83rd and Avalon walk up to a car of Crips caught at the red light and empty a 38 and 22 into the passenger point-blank as he screamed for his homie driving to flee. Hot Dog was supposed to have been watching my back but was always too excited to watch me so neither of us saw the police car ease up with the lights off.

As I commenced the perfected art of reloading, I saw them and ran like my ass was on fire just as the Crip car burned off, and it seemed like for a moment the police were unsure as to whether they should pursue me or the car. The police made the decision to come for me as I dashed through the field then up the alley behind James's spot and over the gate to the house next door, where I paused long enough to stash the pistols, and then kept moving because I knew they would block off the area with one team while the other team searched every yard.

When I made it across 83rd undetected onto 82nd street before the helicopter came, I knew I would get away and by the time I had hit 81st street, I was able to remove my jacket and french braids, throw the empty shell casings into the sewer and cross Avalon to take the alley back up to 83rd where half of the neighborhood stood at the corner waiting to see if the police search would produce me.

When I came from behind to put an arm on Hot Dog's shoulder, his face of guilt and worry lit up with surprise and joy. Then as the bystanders and police began to leave, I suddenly started to feel fear thinking I would die helpless without the guns, so as the last police car departed I slithered to retrieve my stash. Although the police had found the guns, they had left them hidden in the yard on purpose so that they could pounce on me as soon as I went to collect them.

At 17 years old, I ended up in LP in unit E-F for nine months while police worked overtime to charge me with more than gun possessions. However, the judge grew tired of continuing my case based on police promises so with a scolding he told me how lucky I was that the pistols were empty because possession without bullets was a misdemeanor, which carried a six-month sentence for each gun. Therefore, he could only sentence me to one year, which he did, in California Youth Authority (CYA) with nine months credit.

Now again, you would think I'd count this as a blessing and at least think to change some of my vile ways, at the very

133

least acknowledge that something or someone was protecting me for some reason serious enough to make me curious enough to search for meaning, but in my sick and twisted mind, I gave the credit and praise to the gang for teaching me to discard empty shell casings and went off to Karl Holton followed by Y.T.S., an ignorant fool.

The false pretense of being a man because I was "hard" and the vigor in standing for the gang with the infamous reputation for violence toward others convinced me that I was a gangster or a G, but realistically, these labels were only understood by and held meaning to the gang. The world is much, much bigger than your gang, so outside of such, I had no significance and was considered a typical criminal, and people grew intimidated by me. I sit here and now wonder how I ever found this way of living attractive.

In any event, C.Y.A. was no different than LP, and I did what I always did which was to represent the gang and its interests, unaware of even my own. This is because there is no such thing or concept of a part-time gang member or banger, for to a gang banger, the hunt lives on. The pride was birthed from being known for terror as well as terrorizing. That was the gang's primary demand--to maintain a constant rain of harm to those we were taught by the streets in our society and the older homies to oppose.

It is said that to consider oneself in or at war, one has to regard his opponent as an equal warrior, but for a Swan, we considered none as equal, and would eventually hold this same bold arrogance toward each other, which is not surprising since this belief and practice is the bread from which we were groomed, so naturally we'd impose such ideas on one another.

For me, C.Y.A. was a place where I could express the most immaturity, vex, and annoy without regard for consequence since I was only required to do less than four months. As soon as that breezed by, I was released with no parole or probation supervision due to being maxed out. I ran to 83rd where Hot Dog was now in full bloom as a Swan, holding his own on his own, and we continued on our inseparable drive toward representing the gang's interests as daily life functioned.

The only thing impeding this was LAPD Detective Johnson, who was some hotshot responsible for putting a string of homies in LP or prison long before my release. The shootings and murder rate turned up detectives like Johnson who'd built careers in the department off twisting gang members in arrest and conviction. I knew off top to avoid and mislead this dude, but I couldn't for long because, sad to admit, this dude was relentless at being a detective and wasn't afraid to bend the law. But in true honesty, Detective Johnson wasn't the dirty cop type. He'd bend the law, yes, but he wasn't low class enough to flat out break it.

Within my first 30 days of being back, I was confronted by Detective Johnson while walking towards 83rd. Our initial introduction came by him driving up on me then jumping out demanding me to "put your hands on the car," then searching me as he persisted in demand to know "what they call you."

I immediately said, "Sir, am I going to jail?" and pretended to act scared by the mere thought of jail as I gave a fake name and address to a 17-year-old kid I knew in Carson, California.

As his partner ran the alias in the car computer, Johnson demanded to know why I would leave Carson to come to the eastside of Los Angeles and warned me of shootings, murders, and gang wars in this area. He then ordered me into the back seat of his brown Chevy Capri and took me into an alley on 84th street where he demanded who I knew from Swan and when I convinced him that I knew no key members, he insisted that I act as an informant for him to keep him abreast on where guns were stashed and what member carried what caliber pistol. He warned me that if I didn't come through with the information he wanted that he would take me to jail, thinking this was a fear of mine that he could use to extort and control me.

The entire time he talked and threatened me, I was thinking how there was nothing intimidating about him and how utterly desperate he seemed to make a case. I took his card with his private number, pretending to act as one of his recruits as I was freed from the back seat and allowed to leave. I learned how Detective Johnson recruited snitches and informants and how desperate he was to make a case, and I knew I had to be careful with him.

Immediately after coming home, the G-homie Baby Ball, sold me a 38 pistol, which shot 375 bullets, and Ethel sold me a two-shot 357 derringer, which shot 44 bullets, and of course, I went with the largest size slug since sadism drove me--a quality I'd developed from the gang. With my newfound freedom, I did exactly what I always did since I thought it was expected of me, and lacked the sense to care or hold concern for victims victimized. The entire recognition, praise, or respect I believed I held in the gang came from hurting other people--the more grievous the better.

So one late night in the wee-wees while posted in the back of the apartments on 83rd, I heard women arguing, and then saw my homegirl, After 12, in her burgundy cutlass riding alongside a royal blue cutlass with five women Crips inside. Although After 12 was by herself, she kept demanding the women pull over to fight, but the women wouldn't and yet kept calling After 12 a "slob bitch" while yelling "fuck Swan" repeatedly. As the two pulled up to the red light on 83rd distracted by arguing, I calmly emerged from the shadows, walked to the passenger's door, opened it, and then reached in to snatch the keys from the ignition.

As the women turned from arguing with After 12 to see me, they realized what I'd done, and screamed and pleaded "please." I told them to get out because I only wanted the Dayton rims off the car. After 12 suddenly appeared at the driver's window, she pulled on the door handle while encouraging the driver to "gone get out and take this ass whooping" laughing. With every taunt, the driver offered to do anything I wanted if I'd save them.

Worried that the police would come, I pulled out my 38, grabbed the passenger by her braided weave and pulled her from the seat into the street where she began to scratch and scream, so I shot her in the face. Pointing the gun directly at the driver, I again ordered, "get out," and this time they all complied, exiting to my side of the vehicle, which sent After 12 mad. As she ran to my side, she took the gun I released and began shooting the remaining women as they tried to run.

After 12 followed me to where I stripped the car of the rims and the sound system. I replaced the stripped rims with basic tires and drove the car to be abandoned in some rival's neighborhood. Around 6 a.m. that morning, After 12 would demand me to "get out" of her car because I only gave her $200 from the $1,100 Scott LA Rock gave me for the merchandise. I figured she won because initially, all she wanted was to fight, and because of me she got something better plus $200, and yet complained.

Later in the afternoon, I decided to treat my homies with drinks as we gathered on 83rd, so I rode a beach cruiser bike, with Beagle on the handlebars, to the neighborhood store, and as we were leaving with Beagle holding a bag containing close to a $100 of various alcoholic drinks, a car rode by in traffic, and the passenger yelled "fuck Swan" as he spat at us. When I noticed that the car was caught in the traffic jam at the red light on 83rd, I pumped the bike from 81st street, determined to catch up to them before the light signaled green as Beagle held on, insisting that I wouldn't make it in time. As I reached 83rd at fast speed, I jumped off the bike, ran into the street, up to the lingering vehicle to surprise the passenger, and as he yelled "no, no," I shot him three times with the 38 just as Beagle went off the curb, in the air, landing on his feet as the bag of drinks crashed to the ground.

After a few days passed by, the homies and I were posted on a less conspicuous block smoking weed to avoid dispute or disruption, when Detective Johnson raced up, jumped out, and told everyone to leave as he handcuffed me, repeating "Bleep" over and over as he searched me, finding nothing. He told me that I was a good liar and an excellent actor, which revealed that he was upset at being duped during our initial introduction, and maybe even took it personal.

As he took my picture for his gang file book, I went on a rant when he wrote "Bleep" on the polaroid, insisting that my name was "Master Blaster" not Bleep. When he switched the name, I smiled to myself, believing my deceit somehow gave me some advantage that I could exploit later.

Detective Johnson then forced me into the back seat of his Capri and drove towards Watts, all the while telling me that shootings had spiked since my release from C.Y.A.. He demanded that I answer any questions he had concerning various gang shootings and killings that Swans were suspected of, the whole time calling me "Master Blaster," which for some reason tickled me pink. But that humor quickly faded as he pulled in the entrance of the Jordan Downs projects, got out to unhandcuff me, then drove off leaving me abandoned in Crip territory. Luckily, I was able to catch a bus and make it back to 83rd without incident, but the entire experience reinforced my resentment toward Detective Johnson and the law.

Over the next few weeks, Detective Johnson would show my picture at every shooting or murder scene, but I

142

learned his schedule and knew when to get off the streets to avoid him altogether. He began sending messages through homies he managed to catch, reminding me that although I didn't see him, he was there watching and waiting to put me in prison, which didn't phase me because I was much too obsessed with serving the gang and its purpose all while still under the illusion that gang culture could or would protect me.

For almost six months I was able to avoid contact with Detective Johnson who was always near until one afternoon while on 79th and Avalon, in the cut where Hot Dog once dueled with the F13 Mexican soldier, about 20-30 homies gathered in the dairy market parking lot next door. While engaged in banter, a car with three Crips in it cruised by inconspicuously, then went up the street and made a u-turn as the back seat passenger prepared to shoot while the driver made a second pass. But before reaching the crowd of Swans, they had to pass me, and before they did, I stepped into the street to open fire with my 38 at the oncoming car. Focusing on the back seat gunman, my first shots took him out and as he went down in the seat, the front seat passenger reached back to retrieve the gun and began shooting wildly at me as I took cover behind a parked car to reload. I was programmed and trained to count shots fired at me in shootouts, so when the shooter shot past 10, I knew he either had a 16 or 21 shot nine millimeter. By his 16th shot, I was ready to spring and unload again, and as I let off about three shots, I saw a Chevy Capri at the stoplight on 79th and knew it was Detective Johnson.

As soon as I heard the engine rev, for a brief moment I experienced deja vu considering that I just got out of jail for this exact same act, but that realization made me run that much harder to evade Johnson's grasp. I knew Detective Johnson was pissed off because, for one, he couldn't catch me, and two, he told everyone I was wanted for a gang murder and anyone who helped me would go to jail too. He especially threatened Hot Dog, but after two weeks when mom's house wasn't raided with a warrant for my arrest, I knew Detective Johnson was full of shit and just mad because he couldn't arrest me, so I avoided him, hoping he'd go away--but not a chance.

For two months I lived in the shadows, then one day as Hot Dog routinely said, "here he come," I didn't run or hide because I no longer wanted to, and wanted to make that clear. So when Detective Johnson pulled up, he seemed surprised that I was there, then calmly got out of his car, went to the trunk, took out a shotgun, came to where I was on the porch, put the barrel of the gun on top of my head, and dared me to run. He then made me lay prone in the dirt, and before handcuffing me, went to put the shotgun back in the trunk, taking his time, hoping that I'd run so he could shoot me. When he did handcuff me to put me in the back seat, I told Hot Dog with confidence that I would be back.

Detective Johnson first drove me on 61st and San Pedro Ave to some apartments the East Coast Crips controlled and operated, and as soon as he parked out front, he told me that if I didn't give him the gun I used to shoot up the car on 79th and Avalon that he would offer me up to the Crips here who he well knew were arch-enemies of Swans. When I denied being a shooter or having the mere knowledge of a gun, Detective

Johnson turned on the speaker and announced through the radio system that he had a Swan named Bleep in the back seat responsible for shooting many of them, and slowly like skeptical squirrels, Crips began to come towards the car.

When they saw me, the ones who recognized me referred to me as "that's one of them," then begged Detective Johnson to turn me over. I knew he wouldn't, so when he got out of the car, I focused on memorizing those faces for future encounters. After about 10-15 minutes, there were at least 50 Crips trying to convince Detective Johnson to release me. Suddenly he said, "I can't do that," and drove me to the 77th police station where he held me for 72 hours while desperately trying to find the Crips that I had previously shot it out with through reported gunshot wounds.

At the end of the 72 hours, Detective Johnson took me to the intersection of Florence Ave and Avalon Blvd next to the hardware store and told me his car got so dirty chasing after me that he wanted me to wash it before letting me go. The phrase "letting me go" gave me the motivation to wash his car spick and span clean, and now that I think back on this event, I was better off detained because I was being let go into a world of nothing.

At least while detained I was forced to feel worry, concern, or perhaps fear, some type of emotion as opposed to the hard heartless act that the gang crafts in all its members. The level of risk I had grown so accustomed to taking was evidence in itself that I was beyond reckless and more than willing to sacrifice my future, freedom, and life in something that can only be described as a suicidal roulette, but with odds that could only ensure I'd lose. The only way I could have possibly lived and thrived in such dangers without considering this likely outcome was if I was under some deluded belief in arrogance as a result of what the gang made me think I was and who I actually was, or if I just didn't care about anything or anyone, not even myself.

The similarities between gang members and military recruits are striking, as both declare to uphold and defend, and take immeasurable risks in order to do so. The nobleness may surely differ, but the sense of pride and dedication are one, and the loss of lives to one's cause only reinforces the notion to avenge, defend, and represent.

The military produces the image of what some call men, soldiers, and warriors; the gang compels and positions boys to endure acts which most men would find troubling, producing murderers and criminals. While the military promotes honor in fighting for others' freedoms and tranquility, the gang's promotion of honor comes from victimizing and slaughtering one's own neighbor and others like us lost in the struggle. So in considering the attraction to something so debauched and sinister, one has to consider the concept of forbidden fruit as being the most tempting and the values, morals, and principles installed by parents or caregivers. For me, it was: "if someone hits you, you better hit them back, and if you can't beat them you better pick up something and go upside they head," or "boys don't hit girls," or "you better not let nobody take your stuff, you better fight," and "if you get beat up, don't come home."

I had to confront and resolve my confusion and fear of fear itself by not only welcoming it but also embracing it, as to then turn that fear into energy, and once I became comfortable with this, I learned to hide and tame that fear behind violence. With these beliefs and practices, I was a prime recruit for a gang long before I was accepted into one because the predisposition to violence had already taught me that under particular circumstances it was alright, or even warranted, to hurt others. The gang culture took this belief and practice, as well as my own confusion, and expanded on it, giving me even more reason and excuse to harm others. Instead of in defense or to protect, it was simply to terrorize and intimidate to glorify the gang.

To further demonstrate how gang culture rendered me some imbecile, I well knew Detective Johnson's motives and intentions. I was strongly aware of the fact that he was hired and paid by the city to target people like me, and that he was looking to incarcerate me. Yet despite his repeated admonishment and the bizarre fortune to have escaped his grasp thus far, I continued to disregard, mock, and challenge his ability to do his job by continuing to shoot that gun. And so, in the mid-1990s, while ordering from Jimbos in the early afternoon, my homie Big Chops and I watched as a male and three female Crips came walking by, obviously scared from knowing that they were in the wrong area. Big Chops asked me for the gun, but I assured him that I'd handle it, so he got into his 69 Chevy and departed.

I confronted the members on the corner of 82nd and Avalon, and despite being dressed in blue, the guy swore that he merely liked the color and wasn't a Crip, but one of the girls in a blue sports jacket got angry and snapped at me to defend the guy. I pulled out my gun and hit her in the head with it, then made her take off her oversized jacket as I hung it on the light pole and set it on fire.

As the jacket burned, I challenged the guy for allowing the girl to act harder than him. I then tried to shoot the guy in the face which he somehow anticipated in time to duck and run into ongoing traffic as I shot at him twice more, wounding his torso, and as he fell his female protector ran to his aid as car horns blazed.

With all of the sudden attention, I began walking up 82nd street before seeing a motorist stop to pick up the wounded guy and the girl. As I made it to the mouth of the alley to reload, one of the two girls left on the corner appeared and confessed that they were 69 East Coast Crips whose car stalled and that she liked me because I reminded her of a predominant East Coast Crip named Morestein who was wanted dead by many Blood gangs. Interested in the fact that she knew Morestein, excited by her promiscuous wit and attracted by her lack of fear, I invited her to a vacant apartment we used as a spot, and she convinced the remaining girl to come along, who agreed as long as I didn't shoot her.

After smoking weed, they wanted beer, so I left to go buy some, and once drunk, the promiscuous one, who introduced herself as Nasty, began touching me and pulling at my pants until we decided to enter one of the bedrooms where Nasty took me with her mouth for over an hour while her friend waited impatiently. After about three hours of shelter, I drove them to 102nd and Avalon, took Nasty's phone number, and promised to introduce her friend to Hot Dog.

When I made it back to 83rd, Detective Johnson awaited me with a big smile on his face. The girl I hit with the gun was in his back seat and identified me as the one who burned her jacket, hit her with a gun, and shot her boyfriend. I immediately began to run to try and hide the gun and to escape, but Detective Johnson expected such and had back up police officers release a police dog to bite me into surrender and submission.

Since I was 19, I was taken to the Los Angeles County Jail on an array of charges like attempted murder, assault with a weapon, battery, robbery, kidnapping, and gun possession, to name a few, but after nine months, I took an erroneous plea deal for forceable oral copulation and 2nd-degree robbery, out of fear that police would find the Crip that I shot and force him to testify. Despite the oral sex between Nasty and I being consensual, as her testimony also proved as such, I still took a plea to dispose of the entire case in order to avoid a conviction for shooting someone, which was just as stupid as being in a gang.

I pleaded guilty to something I didn't do and went to prison for 18 months to evade responsibility for something that I actually did. Only the ignorance of a gang member could rationalize or make sense of such a foolish decision, and that's due to the many foolish acts one becomes so accustomed to carrying out for the gang. This should have also shown me what low regard the justice system and a civilized society had for gang members in general. Perhaps the embarrassment in itself would have been enough to shame me with indignity, leaving me desperate to change my ways of living, but sad to say, I went off to prison for the first time believing that I had won or gotten away with something.

By this time, I had yet to reach the height of my career as a gang member, so quite naturally I could go on with tale upon tale of escapades in furtherance of the gang's interests, but at this point to do so would be to glorify its image. I only disclosed what I did so those trapped in a gang may know that I relate from personal experience and am not only serious but accurate as I conclude this book "The Hell With a Gang."

For many gang members, there are unfortunate situations or circumstances that cause them to disown or be disowned by the gang, either because they somehow betray the gang or the gang betrays them. In my case, I didn't drop or wash out, wasn't forced out, and didn't leave in bad taste.

Somewhere between the age of 35 and 45, I suddenly grew disgusted with my ruined life and only had myself and the gang to blame. When I became fortunate enough to meet people outside the gang culture, I realized other interests and strengths I had which the gang had no use for and never developed.

As I built up these strengths on my own, I developed more resentment toward gang culture since I clearly saw how I spent so much of my life representing the gang's interests that I never knew or cared for on my own. This is the perfect definition of a waste and being used--it threatens the sound

154

sense of my sanity to reflect back on just how gullible I was by gang culture to have willingly allowed the gang demands to take priority over my own personal growth and development, reducing and limiting me to nothing more than a criminal.

The only way by which to soothe my resentment and maintain my overall sanity is by sternly declaring "The Hell With A Gang" and by broadcasting the truth about gang life and culture to all those enslaved by its operative appeal. A gang is a group too ignorant and weak to stand individually, and a homeboy is nothing more than another creep all too willing to throw his life away alongside yours, and if you believe being a gang member or banger makes you hard or important then you are so lacking in substance that you need to believe in a con to save you from being empty and shallow.

To be respected, one has to know and stand firm on morality and not be misled or influenced to abandon such. To be loved, one has to protect life by enriching that, or those which live, and if one desires to be important they need only deter one person from harm or making a mistake. The more people deterred from some form of destruction, the more

important we become, so we don't need a gang to have or hold

status.

Gang culture further compels or positions one to hold

secrets entwined by lies, and I found that the constant

suppression of foul shameful deeds resulted in me having to

spend a lot of energy, time, and effort in perfecting deceit,

neglecting my own hope and dreams as gang culture consumed

me until I was all used up.

The many events throughout my young life all affected

me in a lot of different ways, but what affected me the most was

never being able to talk about how the effects of such violence

made me feel and then having to pretend that I wasn't affected

at all while continuing to do the same things, which caused this

confusion from the effects.

The cycle in itself kept me off balance where I fast

became conditioned and programmed to only do, think, and

say what the gang wanted, caring only for its needs while my

own became secondary.

In deciding to say "The Hell With a Gang," I reclaim my self-worth and independence by separating myself from the gang to stand on my own, taking responsibility for me, my actions, reactions, and inactions. I allowed myself to expand beyond gang culture and what I've found of interest far exceeds anything that a gang could have ever offered, leaving me to only wonder what accomplishments I could have made in life had I not spent decades wrapped in confusion and misguidance. What achievements are now possible now that I've awakened to finally act as my own man?

The mere prospect alone is nothing short of exhilarating, and the false sense of pride from representing a gang could never compare to the genuineness of pride from creating or building something of merit, something of momentous value which others can benefit or even learn from.

If you are in a gang then you should know your life is being wasted in ruin and as long as you need or rely on a crew or gang, then you defy manhood simply because a gang cannot teach you how to stand strong alone--the mere dependence on others to aid in your representation of gang culture cripples the notion of finding comfort in being firm solo.

Although it is true that humans are sociable creatures and benefit from a healthy support system, there is a negative notion towards solitude. But it is through your own company, free of any external opinions or distractions, that you will be able to learn about yourself for the first time.

Embarking on the journey of understanding oneself allows you to pinpoint the roots of your trauma--what caused you to react, think, feel and live a certain way--and while this may have once helped you survive adversity, it now holds you back from a prosperous life. Embracing your own company allows you to think for yourself, discovering what is of genuine importance to you, your likes, dislikes, needs, desires, dreams, and goals in life. And with this self-awareness is the key to the door of liberation, peace, love, fulfillment, healing, growth, success, prosperity, and joy.

If you somehow find a particular gang appealing and are close to succumbing to gang culture and its absurd view or principles then you are about to inflict hurt and destruction onto others before yourself. Know that when the gang is done with you, you'll be left with nothing or no one except the memory of a string of shameful tales of how the gang either influenced or compelled you to wreck your own life for a gang that you'll eventually learn does not care about you since it can't even care for itself. This is evident in the lack of encouragement, support, and morals towards you, which help you to experience peace, health, success, love, a sense of safety, and joy.

The only consistency the gang has is its infliction of trauma onto others, which ultimately causes trauma to oneself. Its morals are rooted in violence and treachery, so that anything of honest sincerity is entirely disregarded and unwelcomed. Instead, the suppression, denial, and ridicule towards having and expressing feelings, as well as desiring, creating, and maintaining loving relationships is fostered. This in itself continues to fuel the ongoing cycle of trauma of "hurt people hurting people," because to love and want to be loved is a human need, to feel emotions is natural, and opposing either of the two is to disconnect yourself from who we truly are, therefore foolishly rejecting that one is human.

Gangs often capitalize on young men and women looking for things they don't often find at home, things like love, connection, community, safety, and strength. But what is found in the gang are superficial linkages tethered to trauma, a mere displacement of what is actually needed in the healthy and wholesome development of a human being. The desire for the superficial is made all the more appealing if in childhood, your feelings, thoughts, and experiences are not validated, heard, or supported. Instead, a natural disconnect occurs--you render your emotions as weak, your experiences as unspeakable. You do not address them and seek external validation for the things desperately missing and needed for your heart.

For many men, this disconnect is furthered by the toxic, perpetuating culture of having (and wanting) to be "hard." To be hard is to separate the self from feeling--to shut off what makes you human. In the absence of a safe space to speak up and be validated in your emotions, you grow up without an understanding of how to communicate or connect with others. And when you do find yourself connecting to your humanness, connecting with and communicating your emotions, you find yourself being ridiculed by others, primarily other males, who are speaking from a wounded place. So to avoid that shame or embarrassment, you go through life with your thoughts and feelings bottled up, distracting yourself to suppress them, invalidating yourself and your experiences in the erroneous attempt to display strength.

But the emotional stuffing of never expressing or displaying your emotions causes a devastating impact, not just in your personal relationships, but also to your body, mental health, and overall well-being. Emotions that are trapped in the body create stagnation, which can result in the body being in a state of dis-ease, creating physical manifestations in an attempt to call your attention to look within yourself and address the matters you've been neglecting, avoiding, and suppressing.

Another by-product of prolonged emotional abandonment and disconnect is anger. Anger is a self-protective mechanism that activates when we feel threatened. Someone who has not been introduced or accustomed to vulnerability can perceive it as a threat because the uncomfortability and uneasiness from being unaccustomed to vulnerability and what comes with it, such as honest communication, revealing difficult or dark parts of ourselves, displaying our emotions or receiving the emotions of others, and asking for or accepting support, can overwhelm and trigger the nervous system.

Once the sympathetic nervous system, which is responsible for our fight or flight response, is activated, anger can arise to protect the individual who feels they may be in harm's way--whether the harm is real or not. However, anger is just a mask for deeper emotions such as grief or fear.

Nonetheless, because anger is one of the most common emotions and methods of communication displayed by those who are disconnected from themselves, it reveals how much healing we need to do individually and collectively, as inflicting harm onto others is unacceptable and a cycle we must be responsible for stopping.

An important factor of growing is coming to an understanding of what you needed as a child, validating those needs, forgiving yourself for not receiving them, and beginning to establish an internal environment where you can provide those things for yourself. Trauma starts when we begin to feel unsafe, but it ends when you validate your thoughts and feelings, allow yourself to be heard, and nurture your inner child to feel loved and safe.

In the end, many of us are simply wounded children in adult bodies. The detachment from ourselves and the lack of self-knowledge leads us astray into a more superficial world where people gain a false sense of validation from material possessions, unhealthy connections, and praise for living inauthentically.

And yet, to live authentically is to embody courage each and every day and to use it to not cause harm to others, but rather to remain honest, kind, compassionate, respectful, mindful, and loving. To do this, we must embark on the journey of reconnection to the self and recognize our patterns, triggers, and the roots of certain behaviors and perspectives. When we are able to do this for ourselves, we can do this for others, helping to further the essential human qualities of being loved, heard, validated, which are all necessary for our growth, healing, and health. Once we understand ourselves, we can begin to understand others, increasing empathy and love for other people to ultimately make the world a safer, better place.

There is no need to have to experience the devastating after-effects of gang culture, and especially so when I am here as a surviving witness to attest to its gruesome end. In the aftermath of the generation of homeboys who influenced and groomed me to bang, 50% are dead, add to this collection of Big Bop, Chuck, Big Fats, Ice Man Morgan, Poo Bear, Rontoe, Ice 'B', Moon, Dray, Angel, Pete, Dog, Rub, Hot Dog, Big Noon, Tommy Joe, After 12, Lil Lump, Moe, Gizmo, Black Bird, Baby Ball, Sinnister, Froot Loop, Ace Kapone, Pacman,

164

X-ray, D. Rock, Fat Charles, Nate, Sticky Rick, Crow, Blass, Lil Sike, Whip It, Chubbs, Elvis, Big Regg, Tone, Pete, Weebowabble, Stomp, Baldy, and Al Dog, to name a few obituaries. Anyone may fathom how I suddenly bask in feeling blessed just to have escaped with my own life.

The other 40% are imprisoned for life, 6% have become the new neighborhood homeless addicted to some form of drug, and the other 4% were wise, fortunate, or lucky enough to accept their wounded scars and escape with their life to some out-of-state place and never look back. I intend to be among the rare percentage devoted to tearing down what I helped build, commencing with this sonorous "The Hell With A Gang."

As a survivor of this devastation, peppered by layers of pain and endless scars of trauma, I took the only positive skill learned in the gang, and that's how to survive, and I used it to collect myself from the rubble, thereby seeking forgiveness from a higher power and then forgiving myself. And in that forgiveness, I discovered that the compassion and love I held for people as a kid was there all along, but dormant underneath clutters of anger, confusion, resentment, pain, and that hunger for violence which strangely enough acted as the seal to conceal the former. Violence became the mask which hid compassion, and it was only when I removed the disguise that I was able to recall who I am and reclaim my true self.

Therefore, it is in the truest form I come to share the mechanism of gang culture--the loss, the sorrows, and all its pains--in hopes of not just displaying what the outcome of gang life will undoubtedly bring to any involved, but more so with the intention to inspire courage, vulnerability, and accountability to rant "The Hell With A Gang."

Glossary:

Banging: the process of representing one's gang through primarily illegal, violent acts

Best Chum: best friend; a close pal

Buss on: to shoot

Buster: a term used to identify someone timid, unable, or unwilling to uphold gang expectations

Catted: a term used to reference someone who didn't honor their word and backed out

Chamber: the part of a gun in which the bullet is loaded into

Chow: referring to a meal or food

Crabs: an insulting term primarily used by Blood gang members to disrespect and/or identify rival members

"Duck Huntin'": a term used primarily by East Coast Crips which means to target and shoot Swan Blood gang members

G-ride: a stolen vehicle

Hard: a misconstrued belief of being tough, rugged, or invincible

Heat: a slang term for guns

"Keep Them Spots Jumpin": a phrase used to refer to the importance of keeping one's illegal business operating

Kitchen Crips: the name of a Crip gang located in South Central Los Angeles

"Lace Me": a phrase which means to enlighten, educate, or bring someone up-to-date

"Look Scary": to look weak or cowardly

"Put in Work": to kill or harm others in furtherance of a gang

Sister: an African American woman

Slippin': to be caught off guard; not paying attention to your surroundings

Slob: a derogatory term that Crip gang members call Blood gang members in disrespect

Slugs: bullets

Snitch: a person who gives up information, primarily to law enforcement, in exchange for leniency

Wee Wees: a term used to identify the time between late hours of the night and the early hours of the morning

"What that Swan like?": a self-reassuring phrase used by a particular gang to intimidate others, to boast and/or to motivate self